3/6

MORE ESSAYS OF TO-DAY ❧ ❧ ❧ ❧

THE HARRAP LIBRARY

A full list of the series will be sent on request

J. Morton Sale

MORE ESSAYS
OF TO-DAY

Selected by F. H. PRITCHARD

LONDON: GEORGE G.
HARRAP & CO. LTD.
39–41 PARKER ST. KINGSWAY
BOMBAY AND SYDNEY

First published 1928
by GEORGE G. HARRAP & Co. LTD.
39-41 Parker Street, Kingsway, London, W.C.2

Printed in Great Britain
by Robert MacLehose & Co. Limited
at the University Press, Glasgow

PREFACE

IN the previous volume, *Essays of To-day*, the compiler regretted that, in the nature of things, he was able to offer but a very little of the great wealth of material that was available. The call for a second volume enables him to rectify this to some extent at least, and as no writer who was represented in the earlier volume is included here, it will be seen that the two books are complementary, and together give examples of the work of sixty-eight contemporary essayists.

For permission to use the essays in the present collection thanks are tendered to all the authors and publishers concerned, particularly to Mr J. C. Squire and Messrs William Heinemann, Ltd., for "Moving a Library," from *Books in General*; to the Rev. J. O. Hannay, D.D. ("George A. Birmingham") and Messrs Methuen and Co., Ltd., for "Asking Questions," from *Spillikins*; to Mr A. P. Herbert and Messrs Methuen and Co., Ltd., for "The Art of Drawing," from *Light Articles Only*; to Dr George Saintsbury and Messrs Macmillan and Co., Ltd., for "Grasshoppers," from *A Last Scrap Book*; to Mr B. Macdonald Hastings for "The Apotheosis of Dough"; to "The Londoner" and Messrs Cassell and Co., Ltd., for "The Malignant Coin," from *Day In and Day Out*; to Mr Philip Guedalla and Messrs Hodder and Stoughton, Ltd., for "Fez," from *A Gallery* and *Still Life*; to Messrs Methuen and Co., Ltd., for Mrs J. L.

Garvin's "Drowned Bells," from *As You See It*; to Mr Stephen Gwynn and the Talbot Press for "A Sunday in Donegal," from *For Second Reading*; to Mr George W. Russell ("Æ") and Messrs Macmillan and Co., Ltd., for "On an Irish Hill," from *Imaginations and Reveries*; to Mr Charles Whibley and Messrs William Blackwood and Sons, Ltd., for "New York," from *American Sketches*; to Mr G. S. Street and Messrs Constable and Co., Ltd., for "The Shops and Taverns of Piccadilly," from *The Ghosts of Piccadilly*; to Mr Stephen Graham and Messrs Macmillan and Co., Ltd., for "Sunset from the Gate of Baidari," from *A Tramp's Sketches*; to Mr John Masefield for "Niagara," from *Recent Prose* (William Heinemann, Ltd.); to Mr Osbert Sitwell and Messrs Gerald Duckworth and Co., Ltd., for "Round Etna," from *Discursions on Travel, Art, and Life*; to the Literary Executor of the late Mrs Hubert Bland for "About Happiness," from *Essays by Hubert*; to Mr J. B. Priestley for "On Doing Nothing"; to the Very Rev. Dean Inge and Messrs G. P. Putnam's Sons, Ltd., for "Letter-writing," from *Lay Thoughts of a Dean*; to Mrs Jerome K. Jerome and Messrs J. W. Arrowsmith, Ltd., for "On Being Hard Up," from *The Idle Thoughts of an Idle Fellow*; to Mr Gerald Bullett for "The Toy Theatre"; to Messrs John Murray for "Home for the Holidays," from J. T. St Loe Strachey's *From Grave to Gay*; to Mr Gerald Gould and Messrs Methuen and Co., Ltd., for "On Going Back," from *The Return to the Cabbage*; to Mr Ivor Brown and Mr R. Cobden-Sanderson for "A Sentimental Journey," from *Masques and Phases*; to Mr Alec Waugh and the Cayme Press, Ltd., for "London in August," from *On Doing What One Likes*; to Mr James Milne and Messrs John Lane The

Bodley Head, Ltd., for " A War Spring in Hyde Park," from *A New Tale of Two Cities* ; to Mr R. S. Hooper and Messrs John Lane The Bodley Head, Ltd., for " Septemberitis," from *One at a Time* ; to Mr H. J. Massingham and Messrs Ernest Benn, Ltd., for " October Trees and Flowers," from *Untrodden Ways* ; to Mr James Agate for " Likes and Dislikes," from *Responsibility* ; to Mr Allan Monkhouse for " On Having Favourites " ; to Mr Thomas Burke for " Time, Place, and Book " ; to the Viscountess Grey of Fallodon and Messrs Basil Blackwell, Ltd., for "Fables and Folk-lore," from Pamela Grey's *Shepherd's Crowns* ; to Mr Robert Blatchford for " Cinderella " ; to Mr Dion Clayton Calthrop and Messrs Mills and Boon, Ltd., for " The History of the Clothes we Wear," from *Etcetera* ; and to Mr John Freeman and Messrs Hodder and Stoughton, Ltd., for " The English Essayist," from *English Portraits and Essays*.

F. H. P.

CONTENTS

9

THE ART OF LIVING

OF VARIOUS OCCASIONS

AS YOU LIKE IT

INTRODUCTION

IT is not belittling the essays of yesterday to say that those of to-day have a special significance for us. " Michelangelo," as Arthur Clutton-Brock wisely observed, " may be the greatest artist that ever lived ; but if we really care for art, we cannot live in his works ; we want painting and sculpture of our own time to express ourselves, and the production of them is the natural expression of our own love of art." So it is with all forms of expression, the essay not excluded. We do not fail to do justice to the great masters of the past because we insist that only those of our own day, speaking our idiom and sharing with us the burdens proper to our time, can express for us our own relation both to times past and times to come. For better or for worse, they are our spokesmen. It may well be, as Mr Eden Phillpotts asserts with becoming humility, that " Scott's little finger is mightier than the thigh of any one among us men and women who are writing to-day," but it remains true that our time is expressing itself through the labours of those men and women who are now writing, and we must leave it to future ages to draw the inevitable and final comparisons. Excessive adulation of the past at the expense of the present would seem, indeed, as foolish as the systematic neglect of anything that has not been written in the past ten years. Our age may be woefully and unhappily decadent, but our age it must remain, and we shall not improve matters by roundly asserting that it is impossible for any good to come out of it.

The wise reader will do his best to uphold the standards which the older writers have raised. At the same time he will ever be on the alert to appreciate the best work that is being produced in his own day and generation. He will persist in the hope that some of it will be found worthy to endure, but he knows that the day of judgment is not yet, and, warned by the melancholy examples set by departed prophets, he will refrain from hazardous predictions.

We are not showing a lack of veneration for Charles Lamb, for example, if we state that there is much in our present discontents which he could not have foreseen, and that a good deal of what we have to take for granted he would not have understood. That is neither his fault nor ours. It is merely the accident of time, which ordained that he should live in one century and we in another. There is, of course, a deal of common ground. The essentials remain, and one is continually being astonished by the eternal freshness of Plato and of Shakespeare. Were it not so, there could be neither literature nor art in the sense that we know it. It remains true, however, that we alone can know the special problems which life in our time has brought, and for the expression of those problems—our contribution to the literature of the ages—we have to trust to our own writers.

The essays of to-day, then, have an interest of their own, just as the readers of to-day have the best possible equipment for judging those essays. We cannot estimate their ultimate worth, but we can tell whether they present a true or a distorted view of life to-day. Even if the essays are not directly written about life to-day, that will still hold good, for the view of a modern essayist writing of the eighteenth century will inevitably be coloured by his view of life as it is to-day.

Mr A. P. Herbert's whimsical recipe for relief from the tedium of committee-meetings, George A. Birmingham's " mild protest " against the unending inquisitions of the Income Tax collector, Mr Macdonald Hastings' discovery of romance in a machine-bakery—these are all instinct with the present, and reveal experiences that could not have been shared in precisely that way by any of their forerunners. Mr Street's description of the Piccadilly that was would not be nearly so pointed if we were not able to appreciate the contrast to the Piccadilly that is. So, too, Dean Inge's allusion to some of the older letter-writers is made significant by his prefatory statement that letter-writing, as a branch of literature, has apparently had its day.

Criticism of the time is, indeed, the keynote of the essay. We are apt to lose sight of this because we so often allow ourselves to be deceived by the labels that we use. Dr Johnson is dubbed a bear and Elia is termed gentle, and we imagine that the matter ends there. These two writers, at any rate, are carefully pigeon-holed, and should be counted on to give no more trouble. And since Charles Lamb has come to be popularly regarded as the typical English essayist we find ourselves regarding the essay as a sweet, discursive, inconsequent sort of affair that leads nowhere in particular. It is, according to this view, a pleasant bypath meadow which is delightful for idle hours, but its seductions are like to prove a hindrance when the call comes for action.

This has all the subtle danger of a half-truth. It is true that it is not the business of the essayist to argue, nor to exhort, and that he is not called upon to exhibit his knowledge or to explain hidden mysteries. The essay, Mr Orlo Williams says, "should set out to prove nothing," and so far the popular view is right, but he adds at the same time that it "may illuminate anything," and here the popular view is often wanting. For it is just in this matter of illumination that the essayist justifies his existence. Not setting out with any exalted notions of his mission, he nevertheless contrives by good humour and rare insight to light up some phase of our life so that we are able to see it in something like its true proportions. So Addison did more to reveal the eighteenth century to itself than all the pamphleteers, and so the essayists of to-day can tell us more of ourselves than we may learn from noisy harangues at street corners or special pleadings in the Press. Our essayist may be gentle, but he is also a rebel, and his rebellion is the more effective because it finds expression in a manner so calm and quiet. If he is a good essayist he never loses either his sense of proportion or his sense of humour, and it is these qualities which make his work such delightful reading and so subtly dangerous to ignorance and all manner of abuses. " The world," Mr Thomas Burke tells us, " will never be remoulded by politicians or scholars or parading preachers. Whatever of fairness it holds to-day has been given to it by the artists, the creators of ideas, the dreamers of beauty." And in this beneficent and very necessary work the essayists have their part.

WORK AND PLAY

MOVING A LIBRARY

J. C. SQUIRE

I DO not remember that any of our meditative essayists has written on the subject of Moving One's Books. If such an essay exists I should be glad to go to it for sympathy and consolation. For I have just moved from one room to another, in which I devoutly hope that I shall end my days, though (as Mr Asquith would put it in his rounded way) "at a later, rather than at an earlier, date." Night after night I have spent carting down two flights of stairs more books than I ever thought I possessed. Journey after journey, as monotonously regular as the progresses of a train round the Inner Circle : upstairs empty-handed, and downstairs creeping with a decrepit crouch, a tall, crazy, dangerously bulging column of books wedged between my two hands and the indomitable point of my chin. The job simply has to be done ; once it is started there is no escape from it ; but at times during the process one hates books as the slaves who built the Pyramids must have hated public monuments. A strong and bitter book-sickness floods one's soul. How ignominious to be strapped to this ponderous mass of paper, print, and dead men's sentiments ! Would it not be better, finer, braver, to leave the rubbish where it lies and walk out into the world a free, untrammelled, illiterate Superman ? Civilization ! Pah ! But that mood is, I am happy to say, with me ephemeral.

It is generated by the necessity for tedious physical exertion and dies with the need. Nevertheless the actual transport is about the briefest and least harassing of the operations called for. Dusting (or " buffeting the books," as Dr Johnson called it) is a matter of choice. One can easily say to oneself, " These books were banged six months ago " (knowing full well that it was really twelve months ago), and thus decide to postpone the ceremony until everything else has been settled. But the complications of getting one's library straight are still appalling.

Of course, if your shelves are moved bodily it is all right. You can take the books out, lay them on the floor in due order, and restore them to their old places. But otherwise, if you have any sense of congruity and proportion, you are in for a bad time. My own case could not be worse than it is. The room from which I have been expelled was low and square ; the room into which I have been driven is high and L-shaped. None of my old wall-shelves will fit my new walls ; and I have had to erect new ones, more numerous than the old and totally different in shape and arrangement. It is quite impossible to preserve the old plan ; but the devisal of another one brings sweat to the brow. If one happened to be a person who never desired to refer to his books the obvious thing to do would be to put the large books into the large shelves and the small ones into the small shelves, and then go and smoke a self-satisfied pipe against the nearest post. But to a man who prefers to know where every book is, and who possesses, moreover, a sense of system and wishes everything to be in surroundings proper to its own qualities,

this is not possible. Even an unsystematic man must
choose to add a classification by subject to the com-
pulsory classification by size ; and, in my case, there
is an added difficulty produced by a strong hankering
for some sort of chronological order. There is nothing
like that for easy reference. If you know that Beowulf
will be at the left-hand end of the shelf that he fits,
and Julia Ward, the Sweet Singer of Michigan, at
the right-hand end, you save yourself a good deal
of time. But when your new compartments do not
fit your old sections, when the large books of Stodge
are so numerous as to insist upon intruding into the
shelves reserved for large books of Pure Literature,
and the duodecimos of Foreign Verse surge in a tidal
wave over the preserves of the small books on Free
Trade, Ethics, and Palæontology, one is reduced to
the verge of despair. That is where I am at this
moment; sitting in the midst of a large floor covered
with sawdust, white distemper, nails, tobacco-ash,
burnt matches, and the Greatest Works of the World's
Greatest Masters. Fortunately, in Ruskin's words,
" I don't suppose I shall do it again for months and
months and months."

From "Books in General"

ASKING QUESTIONS

GEORGE A. BIRMINGHAM

THERE is nothing easier, few things pleasanter, than denouncing other people's vices; and there is always a feeling in our minds that we sometimes manage to

> Compound for sins we are inclined to
> By damning those we have no mind to.

We ought, if we damn sins at all, to damn our own, if only for this reason, that we cannot properly understand the fall of those whose temptations we have never felt. The man who does not enjoy the captivating stimulant of a glass of port should be the very last to denounce the poor dipsomaniac. Burns is perfectly right in saying that " High exalted godly dames " who are " nae temptation " should refrain from giving bad names to their sisters who are. I try, even in the pulpit, where such reticence is particularly difficult, to avoid the fault condemned by the poets I have quoted. I think I may claim to be fairly successful, not because I am singularly virtuous, but because I am not. There is hardly a sin which I need refrain from denouncing, for there are very few—at the moment I can only think of one—that " I have no mind to."

Yet there is one. I have never in my life been tempted to issue a *questionnaire*. The fact that I am forced to use this word—there being no English equivalent—proves that the thing itself is of foreign

origin and that the vice is not native with us. That
the word has a secondary meaning among the French,
' torturer,' shows what they think of it.

I do not, I can say honestly, understand the lure
of this kind of wickedness. I trust that I shall not
be accused of pharisaical self-righteousness when I
say that if the devil came to me to-morrow and offered
me the opportunity of asking my neighbours for
written answers to lists of questions I should not have
the slightest difficulty in saying, " *Retro, Satanas!* "
and should find a positive pleasure in flinging his
sheets of foolscap back in his face. I do not want to
torment other people in this particular way. But
many men do; and the vice is becoming more
prevalent. Every year, so it seems to me, more men
fall victims to it, and once a man begins he cannot
stop. As in the case of opium-eaters, each indulgence
results in increased craving, and the habit becomes
confirmed perhaps beyond the hope of remedy.

If, like drink and dope, this vice were a private one,
affecting only the victim, or at most his family and
friends, I should have nothing to say about it. But
the question-asker brings suffering into the lives of
thousands of innocent and defenceless people while
he himself thrives, often indeed being paid a salary for
doing the thing that he ought to be sent to jail for. In
a really well-regulated society he would be hanged.
It seems to me a duty—I have no doubt at all that it
is a pleasure—to utter a mild protest against this vice.

Often the sin is disguised, covered up with an
excuse of some sort, so that it may not appear to be
the hideous thing it is. The Income Tax collector,
for instance, who issues annually one of the most
puzzling of all lists of questions, pretends that he is
simply engaged in collecting money. He does collect

money, of course, and no doubt when he first began his work the collection of money was his sole object. He may even have wanted to collect it with the smallest amount of trouble and worry possible. But of late years he has fallen a victim to the question-asking habit and has taken to asking for information in a peremptory way. Nobody likes paying, of course, but I think that almost every man would rather pay a little more—say an extra five per cent. on his assessment—than fill up the preliminary forms and answer all the questions which follow the return of these documents. The ingenuity displayed by the Inland Revenue officers in devising supplementary questions is a proof, if proof were needed, that these men are the victims of a morbid craving.

I once held possession of two small fields and there-fore became, in the eyes of the Inland Revenue authorities, a farmer. As a farmer I made a careful return of my profits, which as a matter of fact were losses. I set down every quart of milk given by the cows which lived in the fields, every egg laid by the few hens which wandered about, and everything else, down to the smallest details, about those fields. I congratulated myself that my return was absolutely complete and question-proof. I was over-confident. After a couple of days of meditation the collector asked me to state how many tons of coal I had dug up. He knew, and he knew that I knew, that no coal ever had been or ever could be dug up within a hundred miles of my two fields. He had no hope, cannot have had any hope, of making me pay a single penny on the profits of a private coal-mine. He asked the question simply in order to tease ; or, if that seems a harsh thing to say of any man, because he was the victim of a morbid craving.

I am not a highly paid worker, nor am I particularly diligent, but I am convinced that I could earn enough to pay an extra pound or so of Income Tax in the hours which I now spend solving the puzzles set me and answering the questions, like that about coal, which are put to me. There must be thousands of others in the same position. It is—it can only be —because the collection of revenue is a secondary consideration that the thing is done as it is. The fact is that many otherwise worthy civil servants have acquired the habit of asking questions simply for the pleasure of asking them and are the victims of an anti-social vice.

Generally the question-asker tries to excuse himself by saying that he is collecting statistics.

I do not know that the clergy suffer more than other people from being treated as the raw material of statistics. Doctors, I fancy, are in a worse case. Schoolmasters, and all who are connected with the management of schools, suffer severely. I have heard complaints from business men. Hardly anyone escapes. I only use the sufferings of the clergy because I know more about them than I do of any others.

There is a paper, of enormous size, sent annually to the clergy by the National Assembly of the Church of England. I have never actually counted the questions on it, but there must be many hundreds. Among them are nineteen concerned with the contributions made by each parish to a number of religious and charitable societies—nineteen societies with a question for each. Such information is of interest, and perhaps some value, to the parishes and societies concerned. It is of no value whatever to the National Church Assembly. But even if we suppose that the Assembly, out of idle curiosity, desires the information, or thinks it does, how easy it would be to take the reports of the nineteen societies and extract from them the figures that are wanted. Every contribution from every parish is acknowledged by these societies and could be taken from their reports with very little trouble, with perhaps one-fiftieth part of the labour involved by the thousands of separate forms sent in by the clergy. The figures so arrived at would have the further advantage of being correct, which under the present system—I judge by my own returns —they certainly are not.

If the Church Assembly simply wanted information that is the way it would get it. But it does not want information : it wants to indulge the craving for asking questions on sheets of paper and forcing innocent people to answer them. There is no other conceivable explanation of its action.

Of course, a pretence is made that the returns are required for the compilation of statistics. That is what is said to me and doubtless to hundreds of others when we do not fill up the forms. We are told that our negligent indolence is interfering with the compiling of a whole book of statistics. If we really prevented the compiling of statistics we ought to be given medals, or titles (ecclesiastical, of course), or otherwise suitably rewarded. For statistics are not merely useless—they are misleading, far more dangerously misleading even than the speeches of politicians or the advertisements of moneylenders.

This, I think, is indisputable. It has become a proverb that anything can be proved from statistics. A man of ordinary intelligence can, without the slightest difficulty, prove four or five pairs of contradictory propositions from any collection of statistics.

When he has finished another man, also of no more than ordinary intelligence, will easily prove that every one of the first man's conclusions is wrong. It is far better, because less irritating, and therefore less conducive to blasphemy, for a man to lose himself on a road with no sign-posts on it than on one beflagged with hundreds of sign-posts which all tell lies.

But the statistics excuse is no more than a pretence. Probably in the early stages of their disease those who issue *questionnaires* really believe that they are seeking information for statistical purposes. Later on they abandon the pretence and ask their questions merely for the sake of asking them, quite unashamed.

I was for twenty-one years subject to a bishop who asked me my name, on a printed form, every May. There was some excuse for him the first time, though even then he could have found out what he wanted to know, if he really did want to know it, in any clerical directory. The second and even the third time I tried, being a charitable man, to believe that he had forgotten my name, was too poor to buy a directory, and too friendless to be able to borrow one. But as years went on he and I came to know each other well. I often enjoyed his hospitality, dining agreeably in his house. He often dined in mine. We corresponded, and I signed every letter I ever wrote to him. He was a genial and friendly man, in many things quite sensible. Yet for nearly a quarter of a century he went on asking me to write my name down for him once every year. He did not want to know it. He made no pretence that he was going to embody it in a volume of statistics. He was simply an unfortunate victim of the habit of asking questions.

I used to wonder sometimes what would happen if I wrote down that my name was Sanders Sanderson or John Smith. Would he be surprised? Would he, with mild remonstrance, call my attention to an inaccuracy in my return? I fancy not. In all probability he never read a word I wrote for him, my name or anything else.

One does not, of course, play tricks of that kind on bishops. For the sake of their high office and estimable characters we respect them too much to be flippant with them. But I did try a similar experiment once on an Education Office.

It wanted to know the measurements of a schoolroom. The proper way of finding that out was to ask one of its own inspectors, who constantly visited the school and always wrote down its dimensions in a notebook. That, I suppose, did not occur to the clerk who issued the form of inquiry. He sent his question to me. I answered it. The next year he asked it again, and again I answered it. The third year the same question came to me. I was annoyed, and said that the room was the same size as before. This was a perfectly reasonable answer. Schoolrooms are not trees. They do not grow, and nobody could have added a foot or cut a yard off that room without an inspector discovering the fact immediately. That answer was no use. The clerk, who kept his temper all the time, took no notice of it, and went on sending me copies of the question until at last I gave him figures.

But I did not give him the figures I had given him before. I doubled the dimensions of the schoolroom. He appeared to be perfectly satisfied. The next year I doubled them again. He expressed neither surprise nor misgiving. In the course of five or six years that schoolroom became a great deal larger than St Paul's. It was really, according to the figures I gave, an immense building, perhaps the largest in the world. Even a fourteen-year old office-boy would, I thought, be struck by the existence of such a structure in a small village. But the education authority remained placidly indifferent. Then I suddenly reduced the size of the room, giving measurements which would have been small for a sentry-box. It would have been impossible to get three children, without a teacher, into that schoolroom. The education authority made no comment at all.

Why was that question asked ? Why was an answer insisted upon ? Clearly no use was ever made of the figures I returned. If statistics had been compiled from them and plotted into a graph the result would have been grotesque. The least intelligent official could not have failed to notice the existence of a schoolroom far bigger than the Albert Hall which shrank in the course of a year to the size of an American tourist's trunk, if he had ever read my returns. There is no explanation of the asking of such questions except the one I have suggested. The men who ask them are " mentally deficient." (The mention of educational authorities suggests this phrase, which is a favourite one of theirs.) They have reached this unhappy state by long indulgence in a seductive vice.

It is, I suppose, hopeless to appeal to the law for protection from the persecutions which quiet and peaceable people endure at the hands of question-askers. But something, if life is not to become in-tolerable, must be done. Year by year the number of these papers of questions increases. Year by year more of our time is wasted in writing answers. Year by year the nervous irritation consequent on wrestling with returns gets worse. Yet it is difficult to see what can be done. I have, as I have already confessed, tried the plan of giving totally incorrect and even grotesque answers. That is no use, for the questioner would just as soon have a wrong answer as a right one. I have tried the plan of saying, " See last year's return," when asked, for instance, for the inscription on a church bell which has remained unaltered for several centuries. That is no use. The questioner could get at the inscription in that way. But it is not the inscription he wants. I have tried putting the foolscap sheets of questions straight into the waste-paper basket and giving no answers at all. That is no use. The questioner pelts me with fresh sheets of foolscap, which is exhausting for the postman ; takes to threatening me, which I do not in the least mind ; he changes his tone and says he is sorry for troubling me, which I do not believe ; finally defeats me by getting a bishop or an archdeacon to appeal to my better nature. Then I give in, wishing very much that I had not got a better nature.

The only remedy I can think of is to kill a few of the people who issue these forms. It would not, I think, be necessary to kill many. Perhaps five or six would be enough. The others, fearing the fate of their fellows, would be cowed into quiescence. Morally I think these executions would be as justifiable as the hanging of murderers, for we should be ridding society of pestilent nuisances.

The difficulty is that we cannot get at the right men to kill. To shoot the local Income Tax collector, for instance, would be unjust, and no good cause is ever helped by injustice. The poor fellow, whom we are greatly tempted to slay, is not responsible for the forms he issues. They come from some one who certainly ought to be killed, but cannot be found. It would, for the same reason, be wrong to plunge a dagger into the heart of a Rural Dean. I have often stood with a long carving-knife in my hand close behind the chair in which an unsuspecting Rural Dean was sitting, a man who, regardless of the laws of hospitality, had handed me a list of questions —handed it to me in my own house just before luncheon. A sense of public duty, rendered acute by a consciousness of private wrong, has prompted me to make an end of him then and there.

I have never done the deed yet, and do not think I ever shall. It is not the fear of consequences that holds me back. If I were hanged afterwards I should become one of the noble army of martyrs, and win that posthumous glory inherited by those who die for the Church and humanity. I should like that. A feeling of pity for the Rural Dean, often an amiable and charming man with a wife and children depending on him, makes me hesitate. While I hesitate my resolution is " sicklied o'er " with the thought that, after all, it is not the Rural Dean's fault. He may even hate the questions as much as I do. There is some one else, some anonymous criminal, who issues the questions to the Rural Dean. If I could get at that man I should—but perhaps it would be better to try to cure him. That might be done if he were shut up in an asylum, like those provided for inebriates, and compelled to work for eight hours every day at a typewriter which had no note of interrogation on any of its keys.

From "Spillikins"

THE ART OF DRAWING

A. P. HERBERT

IT is commonly said that everybody can sing in the bathroom; and this is true. Singing is very easy. Drawing, though, is much more difficult. I have devoted a good deal of time to drawing, one way and another; I have to attend a great many committees and public meetings, and at such functions I find that Drawing is almost the only Art one can satisfactorily pursue during the speeches. One really cannot sing during the speeches; so as a rule I draw. I do not say that I am an expert yet, but after a few more meetings I calculate that I shall know Drawing as well as it can be known.

The first thing, of course, is to get on to a really good committee; and by a good committee I mean a committee that provides decent materials. An ordinary departmental committee is no use : generally they only give you a couple of pages of lined foolscap and no white blotting-paper, and very often the pencils are quite soft. White blotting-paper is essential. I know of no material the spoiling of which gives so much artistic pleasure—except perhaps snow. Indeed, if I was asked to choose between making pencil-marks on a sheet of white blotting-paper and making foot-marks on a sheet of white snow I should be in a quandary.

Much the best committees from the point of view of material are committees about business which meet

at business premises—shipping offices, for choice.
One of the Pacific Lines has the best white blotting-
paper I know ; and the pencils there are a
dream.   I am sure the directors of that firm
are Drawers ; for they always give you two
pencils, one hard for doing noses, and one
soft for doing hair.

FIG. I

When you have selected your committee and
the speeches are well away, the Drawing begins.   Much
the best thing to draw is a man.   Not the chairman,
or Lord Pommery Quint, or any member of the
committee, but just A Man.   Many novices make the

mistake of selecting a subject for their Art
before they begin ; usually they select the
chairman ; and when they find it is more
like Mr Gladstone they are discouraged.
If they had waited a little it could have
been Mr Gladstone officially.

FIG. 2

As a rule I begin with the forehead, and
work down to the chin (Fig. 1).

When I have done the outline I put in the eye.
This is one of the most difficult parts of Drawing ;
one is never quite sure where the eye goes.   If, however, it is not a good eye, a useful tip is to give the
man spectacles ; this generally makes
him a clergyman, but it helps the eye
(Fig. 2).

Now you have to outline the rest of
the head, and this is rather a gamble.
Personally, I go in for *strong* heads
(Fig. 3).

FIG. 3

I am afraid it is not a strong neck ;
I expect he is an author, and is not well fed.   But that
is the worst of strong heads ; they make it so difficult
to join up the chin and the back of the neck.

The next thing to do is to put in the ear ; and once you have done this the rest is easy. Ears are much more difficult than eyes (Fig. 4).

I hope that is right. It seems to me to be a little too far to the southward. But it is done now. And

FIG. 4

once you have put in the ear you can't go back ; not unless you are on a *very* good committee which provides india-rubber as well as pencils.

Now I do the hair. Hair may either be very fuzzy or black, or lightish and thin. It depends chiefly on what sort of pencils are provided. For myself I prefer black hair, because then the parting shows up better (Fig. 5).

Until one draws hair one never realizes what large heads people have. Doing the hair takes the whole of a speech, usually, even one of the chairman's speeches.

This is not one of my best men ; I am sure the ear is in the wrong place. And I am inclined to think he ought to have spectacles. Only then he would be a clergyman, and I have decided that he is Mr Philip Gibbs at the age of twenty. So he must carry on with his eye as it is.

FIG. 5

I find that all my best men face to the west ; it is a curious thing. Sometimes I draw two men facing each other, but the one facing east is always a dud.

There, you see (Fig. 6) ? The one on the right is a Bolshevik ; he has a low forehead and beetling brows—a most unpleasant man. Yet he has a powerful face. The one on the left was meant to be

another Bolshevik, arguing with him. But he has
turned out to be a lady, so I have had to give her a
' bun.' She is a lady solicitor ; but I don't know
how she came to be talking to the Bolshevik.

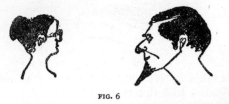

FIG. 6

When you have learned how to do men, the only
other things in Drawing are perspective and landscape.

PERSPECTIVE is great fun : the best thing to do is a
long French road with telegraph-poles (Fig. 7).

FIG. 7

I have put in a fence as well. Unstable, I fear.

LANDSCAPE is chiefly composed of hills and trees.
Trees are the most amusing, especially fluffy trees.

Here is a landscape (Fig. 8).

Somehow or other a man has got into this land-

c

scape ; and, as luck would have it, it is Napoleon. Apart from this it is not a bad landscape.

FIG. 8

But it takes a very long speech to get an ambitious piece of work like this through.

There is one other thing I ought to have said. Never attempt to draw a man front-face. It can't be done.

From "Light Articles Only"

GRASSHOPPERS

GEORGE SAINTSBURY

I ONCE shot a grasshopper, in the garden of a house close to St John's Church, Notting Hill, some seventy years ago. It was the only game that I could ever have hung on the panels, or set stuffed or glazed on the mantel, of my ancestral halls —if I had had any. And this shot was even less intentionally successful than Mr Tupman's at the plump partridge. But the circumstances were rather interesting. The cicala fell to the wadding of a not ignoble instrument, having "got in the way of it," as the defenders of the Manchester assassins said of the luckless policeman and the murderer's bullet. And it was no clumsy cast toy gun—much less catapult or anything of that kind—that impelled the cardboard. Does anybody remember a gunmaker named Blissett, whose shop was in the now destroyed buildings of Holborn? Besides the ordinary stock of his trade, he used to sell most beautiful miniature artillery—not cast, but turned out of genuine gunmetal in exact old naval patterns; carronades with proper breechscrews to elevate or depress, on sliding platforms; elegant little mortars; smaller guns—I forget the proper name for them, is it swivels?—on stands like telescope stands, etc.[1] It was one of the

[1] My father used to give me these on successive birthdays. He also once brought me from the Paris Exhibition (of 1856, was it not?) a miniature *Pièce de Quatre*, the prettiest and completest toy-specimen of H.A. that I ever saw. It was too pretty

35

last named that slew, but not murdered—for there
was no ' intention '—the insect whose Greek forbears
slept and sang " amid the tamarisk's hair."

I should never have slain it intentionally, since it
is in many ways a sacred animal. And I have always
regarded the act as, albeit unintended, sinful and
punishable—difficult, too, to atone for. Perhaps the
punishment, if not the atonement, is taking place
now, as indeed the Book of the Preacher suggests.
Is there *any* greater book than *Ecclesiastes*? Some
people may say, " Oh, this is your Thackeray-mania.
He taught you to admire *Ecclesiastes*." As a matter of
of fact, chronological and other, it was *Ecclesiastes*, at
least partly, that taught me to admire Thackeray.
But that is a detail and a digression.

One has not, unless one is exceptionally κουφόνους,
' light-minded,' to wait to be old in order to know
what the Preacher meant by putting " the grasshopper shall be a burden " in his magnificent and
terrible description of old age itself. But the average
grasshoppers of youth [1] are themselves light, at any
rate passing, and middle age is generally too busy to
pay much attention to its share of them. When one
gets old they have rather a habit of growing to
pterodactyl size, for the moment at least. The shops
won't send the fish you ordered, or the medicine you

to fire and (I strongly suspect) might not have stood that ordeal.
But the Holborn battery consumed plenty of powder in *my* days,
and I think my grandson has some of its constituents now.

   [1] In actual childhood they of course appear—or appear to
appear—crushing ; but children are awful frauds. Their almost
invariable practice of never beginning to cry after a fall, till they
have picked themselves up and found themselves quite un-
damaged, is characteristic. And please let any reader remember
that I do not call really serious disasters, at any time of life,
grasshoppers. They, or some of them, are burdens of a very
different kind—and not momentary.

want. Cigar ash *will* fall on a fluffy waistcoat which has been presented to you by angels. Gratings in the street insist upon snapping off the india-rubber ferule on your stick, and it clatters offensively on the pavement. And in each case the grasshopper, slain a lifetime ago on the top of Notting Hill, avenges itself by being rather bigger and much heavier than an albatross, if not so persistent.

From "A Last Scrap Book"

THE APOTHEOSIS OF DOUGH

BASIL MACDONALD HASTINGS

MY nostrils are steeped in the smell of dough, dough in the kneading, dough in the baking, dough fresh, dough half baked, dough brown and crusty in the mouth. I have spent hours in a great bakery.

Not only has my sense of smell been most pleasantly gratified. My eyes have been enchanted by comely sights, the whiteness of tile and scrubbed wood, the snowiness of bakers' overalls and caps, the lily-tints of cut bread. And for yolk to this egg of exquisite purity and determined hygiene I was shown not only the charming bistres, ochres, sepias, chestnuts, and cinnamons of cottage and tin loaves, French longs, rolls and crescents, but the crocus yellow of Swiss rolls, the straw tints of a hundred thousand cakes, the ruby crests and the mouth-watering chocolates of boy-bemusing pastries.

Not till now did I realize that dough is alive. And I have made bread. I think I make very good bread, but not all my friends who visit me will eat the bread of my baking. So much for friendship! I think that the least a man might do, if he be given roof and couch, is to eat his host's own particular bread. Let those who will not stay in hotels or, like the abbots of old, I will feed them in a guest-house.

Yes, dough is alive. The humane bakers realize this and put it to bed each night covered with blankets.

Moreover, male nurses are kept on duty all night watching lest any of the dough fall out of bed. These tender young men notice at once if Johnny Dough is restless in his vat and likely to tumble over the side. Instantly they go to him, and with firm but tender pressure put him back in his place, afterwards replacing the blanket over his tired figure. It is said that some soft-hearted bakers even imprint a good-night kiss upon the doughy brow, but I did not see it done. No doubt all were shy before the stranger.

The dough is only allowed four and a half hours' restless sleep. Wise men with white faces and blue eyes—why do all bakers have blue eyes, and why is the miller always a tenor singer?—tell me that this is quite enough for him before he is divided up into weights for turning into loaves.

Does dough dream in that sleep from which there is so warm an awakening? And, if he dream, is it of waving corn or a nightmare of human teeth? Dough, I should say, realizes his destiny. All he asks of humanity is to be buttered with English or Imperial butter—and there is no better than that from New Zealand. Please do not spread foreign jams on English bread. You would not if you had seen the proud rising and falling breast of English dough at this bakery of mine.

Three mighty ovens eject two thousand loaves per hour per oven. Six thousand an hour, while you bread-eaters slumber! Ah, if you could but see the eagerness of the loaf to reach you! I shall pass over the somewhat awkward period of the baking. It is no good pretending that the loaf likes it. It is a fact that he goes into the oven weighing 1 lb. 2 oz. and comes out weighing 1 lb. $\frac{1}{2}$ oz. Now when I go to the Turkish bath I enter weighing 13 stone 3 lb., and

leave weighing 13 stone 1½ lb. I suffer, but what is
my loss in proportion to that endured by the loaf?

No. Loaves do not like being baked. In fact,
when they are ready they give themselves away by
positively running out of the oven. They are not
pulled out. In fact, the human hand never touches
them. They come tumbling head over heels on their
moving rollers, laughing and joking and chaffing like
the boys at Eugene Aram's school.

Really, their behaviour is most infectious. I roared
at the sight. This set all the bakers laughing.
People came in from other rooms with inquiring
faces. We pointed to the leaping, frisking, capering
loaves and roared again.

Never was there such a concert of laughter, for
your baker is a jolly soul. But the loaves get little
chance to swap oven stories, and they have a few hot
ones to tell, I'll warrant you. They drop into
wrappers of hygienic transparent paper and take the
rail for the ground floor and delivery-van.

Every one knows that there are brown loaves as
well as white. Then why should I smile when I saw
vats of brown dough? Yet it seems unfamiliar. It
is a sober, russet fellow, and I notice that its loaves
do not frolic as do those of white bread. The brown
loaf sails into the world of mastication on a flat base
and throws not one solitary somersault. It has
dignity and no devilment. I think therefore that you
should not put brown and white bread on the same
platter. Brown bread fancies itself, and association
with the larrikin white must be an almost intolerable
humiliation.

I leave the bread-making for a while and turn for
relief to the inventing of sweet things for the tea-table.
My first thrill is to see the Swiss roll actually roll.

But that is the last stage of his adventure. See him a square, flat slab of brown or yellow cake. He is ready shaped for jamming and rolling. How do they jam him? I ask. Don't tell me that there are machines for spreading jam. Well, there are. There are machines for everything here, including one that cuts bread, butters it, slices ham to fit, and throws sandwiches at you while you wait. The misguided inventor sold the patent of this marvellous machine to his master for £100.

But our Swiss flat is waiting to be jammed before he is turned into a roll. What shall we smear his Little Mary with? Any jam? Any colour? I vote for greengage, because in the jam world I have a greengage mind. A canister of greengage jam is fixed at the head of the machine. The Swiss flats go in at one end dry and come out at the other perfectly and evenly jammed. Now deft young women trim the jam-smeared flats as they pass them on their moving platform. Then they reach the rollers. With not much more than a touch of the hand the Swiss flat is turned into a Swiss roll, and off he rolls and rolls until he falls into a paper wrapper.

I yodelled at the sight, causing some embarrassment thereby to the rolling girls. Why is he called Swiss? I ask. Because the head baker is Scotch, say they. It is the retort cognate, and we beam upon each other.

I have always longed to know something of the home life of the doughnut. He has been with us all our lives, and yet we know no more of him than we do of the extinct fruit and nuts of the past. At school we bought him when we could, and later we knew restaurants and hostesses by the quality of their doughnuts. This delectable ball, with the jolly lump of jam in the middle ! And oh, the delight of the dry sugar on the doughnut's soft brown coat ! Now do they first take the jam and build the pastry round it, and, if not, how do they get the jam into the pastry without making an aperture ?

Well, I saw the doughnuts cooking. They float in a hot syrup, a man standing over them with a long turning-fork. When the bottom side is browned the man gives the ball a touch, and the ball turns. The baked side, you see, is the lightest, and the unbaked side now takes its turn. Next see the browned and cooked doughnut cooled off. Is the jam in ? I ask. Certainly not. He is at present only half a nut, scarcely a nut at all, because he has no kernel. I point out to the doughnut-maker that they are now too late. The nut is whole, and no jam could possibly pass into the ball without breaking it. The friendly doughnutters smile and point to a machine —yet another machine. And what do you think this machine does ? It shoots jam. It is a jam-gun.

The doughnut is put against the wall, for all the world as if he were a spy or a traitor, and the jam-gun torpedoes him. The weapon, loaded with jam, pierces the doughnut's side and then is sharply withdrawn. The jam is left in the doughnut, and, miracle of miracles, there is no sign of a wound in the doughnut's anatomy.

One of the doughnut-makers at my bakery is a man of patriarchal appearance. His mien and his carriage convey his pride in having been the father of millions of dough families. I ask him how many doughnuts he has made. He smiles faintly. Do we take him for Moses, who numbered the children of Israel in the desert of Sinai ?

I ask how long he has been making doughnuts.

Sixty years, says he. When this good man goes his fellows must bake doughnuts and lay them on his grave. The Egyptians believed that the *ka* of the departed needed physical sustenance. Myself, I am arranging for a jar of caviare. Let this patriarch have doughnuts.

This is an age of rolls. If my recollection serves me, bread rolls were rare things in my childhood. They lurked sometimes in railway luncheon-baskets, and I saw them when I was taken to tea with a French nobleman. I turned against them then because the ham of the luncheon-basket was so horrible and because the bearded Frenchman shattered my self-respect by embracing me. Now we eat rolls at every meal.

The story of roll-making is a story of superb machinery, a story of a miraculous overhead railway, and a tale of fastidious hygiene. The little breadlets are scarcely touched by hand from dough-time to delivery-time.

The first machine is a fine, dignified, knowing fellow. He takes the heap of dough into his generous carcass and proceeds to divide it up into correct weights. There is a man I have watched who cuts up steaks all day. He divides the meat so adroitly that each piece is proved by the scale to be of the same weight. A great feat for the human eye and the human hand. But this machine has no eyes, no soul. It is incapable of making mistakes, therefore, and sends out little strips of dough which do not vary in weight by a millionth of an ounce.

The strips of dough, so cut, now move along on their jolly little escalator to the second machine. This fellow is something of a masseur. He picks up the strips of dough and moulds and shapes them on his rollers. He fancies himself as an artist, I should say, so we will not deny him a soul. Certainly he sends away the embryo roll looking very plump and personable.

Now comes the ' proving,' or weighing after mould-ing. For a quarter of an hour the roll travels about. Really, it is the most humane thing, and all roll-eaters should know of it. Before they are baked the rolls are taken for a pleasure trip on a sort of com-bination of the overhead railway in New York City and the scenic at Wembley. They have the happiest time, I guess, and must give each other greeting as they pass and repass on their journey. The speed limit is observed, be it mentioned, and no roll could possibly complain that his nerves were being tried.

Now why are they sent on this trip ? So that during it the yeast may have time to work. What the yeast is doing I do not know, and I do not think anyone else knows. But these master-bakers know at least that a roll which is not given a quarter of an hour's excursion before baking is a fractious fellow. After the journey the rolls take a sort of sausage shape, as if they had been strap-hanging, or, at any rate, sitting seven aside in a carriage. But we know this not to be the case. The rolls are treated from first to last like gentlemen or Pullman-car passengers. They are now turned and sent off again on the moving platforms to be shingled.

The shingling is a pleasing sight. Handsome young bakers stand over the platforms and, while they smile kindly down upon the rolls, give them on the top those three neat little gashes which you know so well. They do this with steel scalpels, but the touch is light and caressing. Air is let into the roll, and one guesses that he needs it. At any rate, he passes on to the oven looking very neat and newly dusted with flour.

I do not know how rolls pass the time in the oven. They are in there for twenty-five minutes, which is a lengthy period in a roll's life, and I have no doubt they make the best of them. I can record, however, that they tumble out when they are cooked with all the gaiety and gambolling tricks of the cottage loaves. They have the same mettle as their parents, and when I pick one up he mischievously stings me with his heat.

Now the rolls flutter downwards through floors and eventually are packed in large paper bags and so made ready for dispatch to all parts of London. Before I leave them I bid one particular roll good-bye. Is he aware of his destination? He may be buttered, he may be jammed, or—horror of horrors —he may be dipped into soup. Will he be broken and left in part upon the plate of a duke so that some of him falls to sparrows or, maybe, the St James's Park ducks? Will he solace a dustman on the dole, or be relished by a pretty chorus-girl between re-hearsals? It is a far cry, in any case, from the corn-field and the nest of the lark.

In the Hall of Dispatch I hover over the loaves, the rolls, and the cakes, and in my head is the thought of a hundred thousand graces. Over this bread a hundred thousand prayers will be offered in the morning.

Men must have known meat-eating before they knew bread-eating, and the original grace was doubt-less offered up to the tribal god when the hunters made an eatable kill. But the grace that we offer up is inspired undoubtedly by gratitude for " our daily bread." I ask you if you were ever inspired to pray by a mutton cutlet or a section of cod. When

I have read a beautiful poem I have felt like saying a prayer. I have seen an Irish priest's hand on his rosary at the start of the Grand National. Every one, consciously or unconsciously, prays when he sees Niagara. But most prayers are said over bread.

Into the night all the food is being hurried, and its fresh, warm colourings will light up thousands of rooms on the morrow, or, strictly speaking, at a later hour this day. It must be a thrilling thought for the bakers that their manufactures inspire prayer in so many homes, that a blessing is called upon their produce daily by men, women, and children.

Look back over your years and reflect upon what bread has meant to you. The first piece you sucked was steeped in gravy or bacon fat, I'll warrant. Then came what is called ' sop,' a mixture of bread and milk, and I hold it a base thing to wet bread. I remember that at school bread was a staple dish. Indeed, we got little else at breakfast and at five o'clock. There was no such thing as tea-time. At five the call was " Bread and beer." We flocked to the refectory and ate chunks of dry white or brown bread, washed down with water if we were little and by ' swipes ' if we were great. So boys are driven to buying doughnuts.

No man has lived who has not eaten bread and butter and cheese with ale in a country cottage on a wet summer day. He must be alone, unless he owns a dog. The wetness of the day needs explaining. I can but say that it has been found that crisp bread has a more luscious taste when the nose is assailed with the fragrance that rises from rain-steeped vegetation.

Take you a couple of crusty loaves, some butter, cheese, and ale, and then buy yourself a cottage.

Preferably it should be at the edge of a wood and a mile at least from the nearest human habitation. Plum- and apple-trees in the garden help, and remind one to deride jam, which, to my thinking, ' goes ' with pastry and not with bread. Sit and slice your loaf, and be neither too parsimonious nor too prodigal with butter. Eat bread-and-butter first and pause. Then eat hunks of cheese and pause. Drink deeply of ale from a large blue and white china mug and pause. . . . Even if you forget the grace before the meal, you will say that appropriate to the end of it.

From the whiteness of bread and the delicate tintings of cake and buns and pastries I walk away into the dark. It is pleasant to think that bread is made in a glitter, though I am glad of the rest to my eyes. I wonder if I would be a baker. Bakers are jolly and they live in that atmosphere which is next to godliness. Moreover, they experience a pleasure which I have hitherto regarded as unattainable. They eat their cake and have it too. Yes, I am a little envious.

In an ideal state I think the chief bread-maker would be a man most highly honoured. In our queer, unbalanced world they give titles and the most money to makers of such little things as plays and books and pictures—to the feeders of the mind. Well, the mind must be fed, but where would your mind be if there were no body to house it ? The master-bakers are puissant because of the power of the Staff of Life. Let them be honoured in accord with their prepotency.

THE MALIGNANT COIN

" THE LONDONER "

AN hour ago I parted from a little friend who has borne me company for this fortnight past. We had lived intimately ; he travelled in my pocket. He was a farthing, and he and I can live no longer together.

Your farthing is like a cock-sparrow for pertness. This farthing had all the qualities of his tribe. I have forgotten how he came to me, but there he lay in my trouser pocket among small coins and keys and trash. I saw a deal of him while the fortnight lasted. Again and again he came up from the depths of my pocket when there was no need of him, as your farthing ever will.

We had not been a day together before he lost me a train. Hurrying down the stairway to the platform I heard a piece of money drop from me and go ringing along the boards. It rang clear as any half-sovereign ever did in the days of peace, when there was gold coinage in England. I was bound to hunt for that ringing thing. The train came in and went without me while I groped and peered for the lost one. Other passengers joined me. When one of them found my farthing and brought it, like an honest man, to its owner, I felt shame. Angrily I put it back among the keys.

After that, not a day without some impish trick of the farthing. Every day it brought me humiliation

by its playful imitation of a sixpence. I have offered
it at the ticket office of the Tube ; I have tried to pay
for my cup of tea with my farthing. Truly I know
now how it feels to be a passer of false coin and to
have failed at the job. Eyes have looked at me
stonily ; the cold courtesy of the young lady in the
money hutch at the tea-shop warned me that the way
of the cheat is hard.

Yet this morning I had clean forgotten my farthing.
It was not until the small boy jeered at me, as I
waited for fivepence in change at the bookstall, that
I remembered it. There was no courtesy about the
small boy ; he gave me no benefit of the doubt. I
tell you that he jeered at me, making a noise of contempt with his mouth.

That was where I left the farthing. Another
plunge of the hand among my keys and I brought up
a true sixpence. How glad I was to see the white
face of it ! I had my paper and my fivepence change
—the boy seemed to count it very slowly, making
sure of it lest I should try to cheat him again. Then
I went away in haste, leaving that accursed farthing
in fitting company, in the company of a grimy boy
who was a sort of human farthing.

He sent a last jeer after me, crying out that I had
left my farthing behind. But I did not turn my head.
I am free and he has the farthing ; I hope it may
bring him to disaster.

There was a man who, writing to the newspaper
last week, asked for a greater coinage of farthings.
That man is our enemy. For why should the Mint
have ever struck these vile pieces that will buy
nothing ?

You know the Mint. A pleasant quarter of the
town is that of the Mint, when the sun is on the

D

ancient walls of the Tower. But it is otherwise when the November mists rise from the river-bank, when clammy darkness holds the east end of the city. Then I can believe that the men of the Mint fall into a sour humour ; they will strike no bright silver for us. Says the master of the Mint, " Come, let us make a batch of farthings."

Nobody has any kindness for a farthing, unless it be a woman. The farthing has no power to vex her ; for woman is an animal without pockets ; she keeps her money in a purse. It is my belief that every woman has at least one farthing in her purse.

Do not ask me to explain why she has a brown farthing in the compartment that holds postage stamps and a receipted bill. It is true that, in the shops where women buy, there are goods marked with prices that end in three farthings. But that is mysterious folk-lore ; it seems as though it were held unlucky for a woman to buy goods at two shillings ; the ticket must be for one shilling and elevenpence three farthings. Yet farthings do not pass over the counter. The small currency is in pins. All that I know is that the woman has the farthing in her purse and that I will never have another in my pocket. A malignant coin it is ; you remember the Queen Anne farthing. It set about a legend of its own rarity, that there were only three of it, each worth a hundred guineas. A man was hanged for robbery on the high-road ; he was after a Queen Anne farthing.

From "Day In and Day Out"

THE CHANGING SCENE

FEZ

PHILIP GUEDALLA

SOMEWHERE in the town a drum was throbbing. The little pulse of sound seemed to go straight up in the silence over the city, like a tall thread of wood smoke into a windless sky. But all round the great place lay out in the still sunshine; and the grey hills, where the olive-trees climb up into the Middle Atlas, looked down on Fez. There is something a little alarming about a city without a sound. When one stands above a town in the West there is always a striking of clocks, a dull thunder of wheels, or the sudden yell of an engine. But down in the little streets which wind through Fez there is no traffic beyond men on foot and sheeted women and the faint click of ambling mules and little donkeys that brush their loads against the walls on either side. That is why scarcely a sound drifts up, as you look out across the city.

It is a grey, congested heap of square-topped houses, filling a whole valley, climbing the little hills, and huddled behind the shelter of the city walls. Tall towers stand up out of the mass, where the *muezzin* goes up between the city and the sky to quaver out the hours of prayer; and beyond the minarets one catches the sudden green of a great roof of tiles. But the memory that will remain is of a heaped grey waste of houses lying silent in the sun. As one stared, it seemed to stare silently back; and somewhere in the town a solitary drum was throbbing.

The little alleys wind in and out among the houses. Sometimes they vanish into tunnels under the piled city, or pick their way across the chessboard shadows of a reed-roofed market. The blue sky comes suddenly round corners, and swarming streets end in the little hill-streams which pour through Fez. There is a sound of rushing water everywhere in the city. It goes whispering under humped Moorish bridges and mutters like a stage conspirator in little strangled tunnels below the heaped grey houses. The great town had seemed so silent from the hills above. But down in the maze, where the veiled women slip discreetly by in the half-darkness of the streets, it is alive with little sounds. Whispering water, the slow lilt of men at work, snatches of high, wailing, minor plainsong (Spain learnt its music at the knees of Africa), low chants from little schools, the tapping hammers of the coppersmiths, are all caught between the tall, blind walls; and the hooded men crouch talking at every corner. The men and the water all talk low. Perhaps that is how Fez muttered ten years ago, before it came yelling down the little streets to murder stray, bewildered Frenchmen in the massacres. In Fez one can never quite forget that spring.

But one day the great city made remarkable holiday. It shut up shop in the early afternoon and went pouring westward up the hill in its best kaleidoscopic clothes. The tide of the traffic set steadily towards the Palace gates. Soldiers, great droves of women, elegant young gentlemen on mules streamed up the little alleys, as tall negroes went elbowing through the press; and solemn citizens, who lie all day in little cupboards three feet square to sell a pinch of green tea for a copper and an hour's conversation, abandoned the excitement of commerce for the keener

joys of spectacle. His Shereefian Majesty was on the
road from Rabat ; and was it not fitting that his city
of Fez should receive the Sultan at the gates ? From
the great square before the Palace there was a steady
roar, and the gorged streets still poured late-comers
into the mass. They stood and pushed and shouted ;
and sometimes, discarding all false dignity, they swept
through the crowd, fifteen abreast, arms linked, knees
up, and singing to the steady thunder of their little
earthenware drums. Above and behind them were
the gates whose great square battlements had so
alarmed the romantic imagination of M. Pierre Loti ;
and somewhere in the middle loud arguments and a
faint gleam of bayonets indicated that anxious French
officers still hoped to keep a road open for the procession.

Royalty was late. But Fez resorted freely to the
consolations of song and dance. Rings formed in the
crowd ; and the little drums throbbed without ceasing, as indomitable loyalists jigged steadily up and
down in line, and hillmen in circles sang interminable
choruses. Then a gun spoke from the green fort
beyond the town, and the heads all turned to the
roadway between the bayonets.

There was something odd about that procession
from the first. It opened with four closed cars, which
glided in perfect silence and with drawn blinds up to
the Palace. There was a roguish intimation that
these contained a selection of the Imperial harem ;
and we gathered from the small number that Majesty
was making only a short stay in Fez. Followed four
open cabs, containing (one heard it with a mild thrill)
the Keepers of the Door, come straight from *The
Arabian Nights* to guard the Sultan's harem. The
misleading art of Ballet had taught one to believe

that these figures of romance would wear a vivacious, almost a festal air ; and to the heated Western imagination those four cabloads of dejected men in pointed red fezzes were a bitter blow. The Sultan of Morocco seemed to have neglected the opportunities afforded to him by M. Bakst. Eunuchs in cabs. . . . One waited gloomily to see a station omnibus full of mutes with bowstrings. But the salutes were still thudding from the battery on the hill, and the infantry in the road sprang suddenly to the " Present." There was a clatter of horses under the great gates ; and a stream of men in white went riding by with long five-foot flintlocks from the Sûs, sitting the great coloured saddles stiffly with feet driven well home into their square stirrups.

Then the colours changed, and negro lancers jingled past in red. Pennons, black faces, scarlet tunics took the procession to the border-line of opera. There was a pause ; and a band launched into the ceremonial discords that are reserved for royal ears. The crowd was roaring in the square ; and when it paused for breath, the shrill *you-you-you*, which squeals for victory or drives men on to kill, came from the women in their corner. The French guns spoke slowly from the battery ; and down in the road, at the centre of the din, a grave bundle of white linen moved deliberately through the noise and watched with unseeing eyes the prostrations of anxious Kaids. For the Sultan had come into his city of Fez.

From "A Gallery" and "Still Life"

DROWNED BELLS

" V " (Mrs J. L. Garvin)

MAY is over East Anglia and its long coast-line fringed with shaggy young corn. A bee rises heavily from the gorse ; a bird drops like a stone into a hedge powdered with white blossom. The two scents, sickly and aromatic, mingle with the salt in the air. A flat, green country set with windmills and channelled by pale arteries of sluggish water. Across the levels, seven grey churches like miniature cathedrals are all visible at once, each rising from its own humble congregation of low red houses. Also it is a still country, and has unseen meanings of things now under the sea. Suddenly, here and there, behind a rare clump of scraggy pine-trees, you get the cold gleam of shallow water in broad streaks. At Dunwich this hungry sea has slowly devoured bit by bit " fifty-two churches and as many windmills, together with a spacious harbour in which there were as many ships as windmills."

Ships and windmills, windmills and ships. The fate of a ship seems naturally uncertain ; it may put into harbour, it may perish. For it is built—as we mortals are—to be a challenging thing, and goes out to adventure, and mishap. But one had not thought it of windmills. That stationary ship, a windmill, standing with open arms, answering to the faintest breeze, yet fundamentally steadfast, seems born saved. Before now one has noted a town with a harbour and one windmill, and counted it rich enough, thankful for its solitary landmark. But under this sea lies a whole social civilization and an ecclesiastical system. Here, the King from Thule might have flung the memory cup to join buried chalices, sunken bells, quenched censers, all studded with mussels now.

Beyond some crooked tombstones at this edge of doom, only a tall needle of the last tower remains. Pell-mell down the sandy cliff topple epitaphs, human bones, shattered coffins. In places the green is already shooting over the scars of last winter's devastation ; while the murky sea of a sandy coast sucks and roars over what might be rocks, but are only the stone corners of the fallen tower. So in their way they " suffer a sea-change into something rich and strange." Soon, soon they also shall be more completely drowned : the last traces of Dunwich and its lost glories shall slip down to join the rest of the legend.

In the hot yellow sand, children in blue and brown are busy digging and excavating. It is like the *Hamlet* scene cheerfully mimicked by the nursery. One cherubic sexton has found a rib, another a branch of white may. One, more ambitious, full of local rumour, drives in his wooden spade with his sand-shoe in gay hopes of a skull.

From "As You See It"

A SUNDAY IN DONEGAL

STEPHEN GWYNN

WE were late in arriving at the old chapel, and the first thing that met us was the sight—less familiar, perhaps, in any other country than in Ireland—of worshippers kneeling outside the open door, unable to find room within. As we passed behind them, we could see the priest in his robes administering the Communion; his figure was silhouetted against daylight, for the door in the south transept also was open, and beyond it the kneeling congregation overflowed on that side also under the sky. Between the priest and us was the huddled mass of women, who sat apart from the men. There was scarcely a hat among them. Shawls and handkerchiefs—red, orange, blue, purple, buff, and brown of every conceivable hue—made such a glow of rich and harmonious colour as you will only see in an Irish-speaking district, where the people still dress in a manner that visibly proclaims their nationality. A friend recognized me, and led us up into the gallery facing the chancel—there were three galleries, and all packed as closely as the seats on the floor. From here we could see the men, not wholly so distinctive in their dress as the women, yet for the most part clad in the rough home-spun, undyed, home-woven frieze. Look where you might, your eyes told you that you were in Ireland ; and I have never been in any other congregation anywhere which seemed to offer such attractions to a painter. What the European countries generally sacrifice, by choosing to wear far-off imitations of what is worn in London and Paris, cannot be counted.

But it was not the eye only that was affected by this evidence of national distinctness. If there be elsewhere congregations so rapt, I have not seen them. For a moment we felt shame at our intrusion, but the fear of having disturbed worship soon passed off ; it seemed as if an earthquake would hardly have broken the spell of that devotion. When the long succession of communicants was done with the priest read the prayers after Mass, not in Latin nor in English, but in the Irish tongue of those he spoke to. Donegal-bred, he had the accent, at least to my unskilled ear ; but he was no native speaker, and when he preached it was in English. All that was needed was the tongue of the people to round off the impression of that discourse. As the young priest stood on the altar-steps, and the old men in their frieze stood by him, touching the very rail, it seemed not so much a religious office as some tribe council where debate was held on matters homely, yet weighty with significance. The Protestant Church, for all its bareness of ritual, has come far away from that primitive simplicity.

Another thing struck me then as never before, for all I have travelled about Ireland—the strength and the constant maintenance, through the church, of the local bond. As the priest disrobed before the sermon, he gave out subjects for prayer : " You will say now a Pater Noster in Irish for all out of this parish who are in America," " A Pater Noster and two Hail Marys for those who are in England or Scotland " (that parish is a great home of emigrant labour),

" a Pater Noster and three Hail Marys in Irish for the dead that are in this churchyard." And the heavy rustle of the whispered prayer would go through the crowded transepts like the noise of leaves on a summer evening—bringing the dead and the far-away very near, it seemed, to those who then called them into memory. Never at any time in Ireland have I felt so remote from England, Scotland, and all the world as there at that Catholic service—so world-wide, yet so homely.

Outside the church door, when benediction ended and no one was left in the building but the school-master teaching children their catechism in Irish, a ritual more distinctive still was enacted. Perhaps fifty out of that immense congregation made their way into the churchyard, and stood for the most part chatting in a group round the monument to a de-parted priest. But a few women there detached themselves from the rest, and, each of them picking her way through the grass to a grave-stone or the little cross that marked a tomb still simpler, knelt down, and, bending forward, pressed her face close to the ground. Then—from the very earth it seemed —there rose a faint crying, hardly louder at first than a cricket's noise—swelling, dying down, swelling again, yet always so faint that out there in the open it was hardly audible ten yards off, unless one strained to hear it. But then a woman raised the chant from a grave just beside us ; and, as one listened to her cry near at hand, and the other faint wailings, all chanted to the same heartrending little tune, they seemed to fill all earth and heaven. It was like the cry, not of this or that wife or mother, but of the land itself—a voice issuing here from among the graves— the wailing of Ireland after her scattered sons. I have heard the keene before from many voices raised together at a funeral, but never elsewhere have I met this weekly renewing of the wail, this melancholy mingling of separate keenings, each mourning its own loss ; and it would break your heart to listen to it.

Away from the church was a very different gathering around the post-office, where men and women crowded and jostled as the postmaster read out names. Well they might look to the post, with the four or five hundred of their men away at the harvesting. It was all a part of the weekly reunion, when these mountaineers and fisher-folk gathered from many miles around have sight and speech of one another. The week centres round Sunday. The church is the meeting point of life for a whole countryside ; and I think the rest of us, not Catholics, who care for Ireland, when we are brought face to face with the Catholic Church at such times and in such places, must feel towards it almost as if it was our own, because it is so deeply interwoven with all the life that is most Irish in Ireland.

From " For Second Reading "

ON AN IRISH HILL

"Æ" (George W. Russell)

IT has been my dream for many years that I might at some time dwell in a cabin on the hillside in this dear and living land of ours, and there I would lay my head in the lap of a serene nature, and be on friendly terms with the winds and mountains who hold enough of unexplored mystery and infinitude to engage me at present. I would not dwell too far from men, for above an enchanted valley, only a morning's walk from the city, is the mountain of my dream. Here, between heaven and earth and my brothers, there might come on me some foretaste of the destiny which the great powers are shaping for us in this isle, the mingling of God and nature and man in a being, one, yet infinite in number. Old tradition has it that there was in our mysterious past such a union, a sympathy between man and the elements so complete, that at every great deed of hero or king the three swelling waves of Fohla responded : the wave of Toth, the wave of Rury, and the long, slow, white, foaming wave of Cleena. O mysterious kinsmen, would that to-day some deed great enough could call forth the thunder of your response once again ! But perhaps he is now rocked in his cradle who will hereafter rock you into joyous foam.

The mountain which I praise has not hitherto been considered one of the sacred places in Eiré, no glittering

tradition hangs about it as a lure ; and indeed I
would not have it considered as one in any special
sense apart from its companions, but I take it here
as a type of what any high place in nature may become for us if well loved ; a haunt of deep peace,
a spot where the Mother lays aside veil after veil,
until at last the great Spirit seems in brooding gentle-
ness to be in the boundless fields alone.   I am not
inspired by that brotherhood which does not overflow
with love into the being of the elements, not hail in
them the same spirit as that which calls us with so
many pathetic and loving voices from the lives of
men.   So I build my dream cabin in hope of this
wider intimacy :

> A cabin on the mountain-side hid in a grassy nook,
> Where door and windows open wide, where friendly stars
>   may look ;
> The rabbit shy can patter in ; the winds may enter free
> Who throng around the mountain throne in living ecstasy.
> And when the sun sets dimmed in eve and purple fills the air,
> I think the Sacred Hazel Tree is dropping berries there
> From starry fruitage waved aloft where Connla's well o'er-
>   flows :
> For sure the immortal waters pour through every wind that
>   blows.
> I think when night towers up aloft and shakes the trembling
>   dew,
> That every high and lonely thought that thrills my being
>   through
> Is but a shining berry dropped down through the purple air,
> And from the magic Tree of Life the fruit falls everywhere.

The Sacred Hazel was the Celtic branch of the Tree
of Life ; its scarlet nuts gave wisdom and inspiration ;
and fed on this ethereal fruit, the ancient Gael grew
to greatness.   Though to-day none eat of the fruit or
drink the purple flood welling from Connla's foun-
tain, I think that the fire which still kindles the Celtic
races was flashed into their blood in that magical

time, and is our heritage from the Druidic past. It is still here, the magic and mystery ; it lingers in the heart of a people to whom their neighbours of another world are frequent visitors in the spirit and over-shadowers of reverie and imagination.

The earth here remembers her past, and to bring about its renewal she whispers with honeyed entreaty and lures with bewitching glamour. At this mountain I speak of it was that our greatest poet, the last and most beautiful voice of Eiré, first found freedom in song, so he tells me : and it was the pleading for a return to herself that this mysterious nature first fluted through his lips :

> Come away, O human child,
> To the woods and waters wild
> With a faery hand in hand :
> For the world's more full of weeping than you can understand.

Away ! yes, yes ; to wander on and on under star-rich skies, ever getting deeper into the net, the love that will not let us rest, the peace above the desire of love. The village lights in heaven and earth, each with their own peculiar hint of home, draw us hither and thither, where it matters not, so the voice calls and the heart-light burns. Some it leads to the crowded ways ; some it draws apart : and the Light knows, and not any other, the need and the way.

If you ask me what has the mountain to do with these inspirations, and whether the singer would not anywhere out of his own soul have made an equal song, I answer to the latter, I think not. In these lofty places the barriers between the sphere of light and the sphere of darkness are fragile, and the con-tinual ecstasy of the high air communicates itself, and I have also heard from others many tales of

E

things seen and heard here which show that the races of the Sidhe are often present. Some have seen below the mountain a blazing heart of light, others have heard the musical beating of a heart, or faery bells, or aerial clashings, and the heart-beings have also spoken ; so it has gathered around itself its own traditions of spiritual romance and adventures of the soul.

Let no one call us dreamers when the mind is awake. If we grew forgetful and felt no more the bitter human struggle—yes. But if we bring to it the hope and courage of those who are assured of the near-by presence and encircling love of the great powers ? I would bring to my mountain the weary spirits who are obscured in the fœtid city where life decays into rottenness ; and call thither those who are in doubt, the pitiful and trembling hearts who are sceptic of any hope, and place them where the dusky vapours of their thought might dissolve in the inner light, and their doubts vanish on the mountain-top where the earthbreath streams away to the vast, when the night glows like a seraph, and the spirit is beset by the evidence of a million of suns to the grandeur of the nature wherein it lives and whose destiny must be its also.

After all, is not this longing but a search for ourselves, and where shall we find ourselves at last ? Not in this land nor wrapped in these garments of an hour, but wearing the robes of space whither these voices out of the illimitable allure us, now with love, and anon with beauty or power. In our past the mighty ones came glittering across the foam of the mystic waters and brought their warriors away.

Perhaps, and this also is my hope, they may again return ; Manannan, on his ocean-sweeping boat, a

living creature, diamond-winged, or Lu, bright as
the dawn, on his fiery steed, manned with tumul-
tuous flame, or some hitherto unknown divinity may
stand suddenly by me on the hill, and hold out the
Silver Branch with white blossoms from the Land of
Youth, and stay me ere I depart with the sung call
as of old :

Tarry thou yet, late lingerer in the twilight's glory ;
Gay are the hills with song : earth's faery children leave
More dim abodes to roam the primrose-hearted eve,
Opening their glimmering lips to breathe some wondrous
      story.
Hush, not a whisper ! Let your heart alone go dreaming.
Dream unto dream may pass : deep in the heart alone
Murmurs the Mighty One his solemn undertone.
Canst thou not see adown the silver cloudland streaming
Rivers of faery light, dewdrop on dewdrop falling,
Starfire of silver flames, lighting the dark beneath ?
And what enraptured hosts burn on the dusky heath !
Come thou away with them for Heaven to Earth is calling.
These are Earth's voice—her answer—spirits thronging.
Come to the Land of Youth : the trees grown heavy there
Drop on the purple wave the starry fruit they bear.
Drink ! the immortal waters quench the spirit's longing.
Art thou not now, bright one, all sorrow past, in elation,
Filled with wild joy, grown brother-hearted with the vast,
Whither thy spirit wending flits the dim stars past
Unto the Light of Lights in burning adoration.

From "Imaginations and Reveries"

NEW YORK

CHARLES WHIBLEY

TO land at Hoboken in a quiet drizzle is to sound the depths of desolation. A raw, half-finished, unkempt street confronts you. Along the roadway, roughly broken into ruts, crawls a sad tram. The dishevelled shops bear odd foreign-looking names upon their fronts, and the dark men who lounge at their doors suggest neither the spirit of hustling nor the grandeur of democracy. It is, in truth, not a street, but the awkward sketch of a street, in which all the colours are blurred and the lines drawn awry. And the sense of desolation is heightened by the memory of the immediate past. You have not yet forgotten the pomp of a great steamship. The gracious harbour of New York is still shining in your mind's eye. If the sentiment of freedom be dear to you, you are fresh from apostrophizing the statue of Liberty, and you may have just whispered to yourself that you are breathing a clearer, larger air. Even the exquisite courtesy of the officer who has invited you in the blandest terms to declare that you have no contraband, has belied the voice of rumour and imparted a glow of satisfaction. And then you are thrown miserably into the leaden despair of Hoboken, and the vision of Liberty herself is effaced.

But Hoboken is an easy place wherefrom to escape, and the traveller may pass through it the more cheerfully, because it prepares him for the manifold and bewildering contrasts of New York. The towns of the Old World have alternations of penury and affluence. In them also picturesque squalor obtrudes itself upon an ugly splendour. But New York, above all other cities, is the city of contrasts. As America is less a country than a collection of countries, so New York is not a city—it is a collection of cities. Here, on the narrow rock which sustains the real metropolis of the United States, is room for men and women of every faith and every race. The advertisements which glitter in the windows or are plastered upon the hoardings suggest that all nationalities meet with an equal and a flattering acceptance. The German regrets his fatherland the less when he finds a brilliant *Bierhalle* waiting for his delight. The Scot no doubt finds the ' domestic ' cigar sweeter to his taste if a portrait of Robert Burns adorns the box from which he takes it. The Jew may be supposed to lose the sense of homesickness when he can read the news of every day in his familiar Yiddish. And it is not only in the contrast of nationalities that New York proves its variety. Though Germans, Italians, and Irish inhabit their own separate quarters and frequent their own separate haunts, there are many other lines of division. Nowhere in the world are there sharper, crueller distinctions of riches and poverty, of intelligence and boorishness, of beauty and ugliness. How, indeed, shall you find a formula for a city which contains within its larger boundaries Fifth Avenue and the Bowery, the Riverside Drive and Brooklyn, Central Park and Coney Island ?

And this contrast of race and character is matched by the diversity of the city's aspect. Its architecture is as various as its inhabitants. In spite of demolition and utility, the history of New York is written brokenly

upon its walls. Here and there you may detect an
ancient frame-house which has escaped the shocks
of time and chance, and still holds its own against its
sturdier neighbours. Nor is the memory of England
wholly obliterated. Is there not a homely sound in
Maiden Lane, a modest thoroughfare not far from
Wall Street? What Englishman can feel wholly
abroad if he walk out to the Battery, or gaze upon
the austere houses of Washington Square? And do
not the two churches of Broadway recall the city of
London, where the masterpieces of Wren are still
hedged about by overshadowing office and frowning
warehouse? St Paul's Chapel, indeed, is English
both in style and origin. It might have been built
in accord with Sir Christopher's own design; and,
flanked by the thirty-two storeys of the Park Row
Building, it has the look of a small and dainty toy.
Though Trinity Church, dedicated to the glory of
God and the Astors, stands in an equally strange
environment, it is less incongruous, as it is less elegant,
than St Paul's. Its spire falls not more than a hundred feet below the surrounding sky-scrapers, and
were it not for its graveyard it might escape notice.
Now its graveyard is one of the wonders of America.
Rich in memories of Colonial days, it is as lucid a
piece of history as survives within the boundaries of
New York. The busy mob of cosmopolitans, intent
upon trusts and monopolies, which passes its time-
worn stones day after day, may find no meaning in
its tranquillity. The wayfarer who is careless of the
hours will obey the ancient counsel and stay a while.
The inscriptions carry him back to the days before
the Revolution, or even into the seventeenth century.
Here lies one Richard Churcher, who died in 1681,
at the tender age of five. And there is buried William

Bradford, who printed the first newspaper that ever
New York saw, the forefather in a long line of the
Yellowest Press on earth. And there is inscribed the
name of John Watts, the last Royal Recorder of
New York. Thus the wayfarer may step from Broadway into the graveyard of a British colony, and forget,
in contemplating the familiar examples of a lapidary
style, that there was a tea-party at Boston.

These contrasts are wayward and accidental. The
hand of chance has been merciful, that is all ; and if
you would fully understand New York's self-conscious
love of incongruity it is elsewhere that you must look.
Walk along the Riverside Drive, framed by nature
to be, what an enthusiast has called it, " the finest
residential avenue in the world." Turn your back
to the houses, and contemplate the noble beauty of
the Hudson River. Look from the terrace of Clare-
mont upon the sunlit scene, and ask yourself whether
Paris herself offers a gayer prospect. And then face
the " high-class residences," and humble your heart.
Nowhere else will you get a clearer vision of the
inappropriateness which is the most devoutly wor-
shipped of New York's idols. The human mind
cannot imagine anything less like " residences "
than these vast blocks of vulgarity. The styles of all
ages and all countries have been recklessly imitated.
The homes of the millionaires are disguised as
churches, as mosques, as medieval castles. Here you
may find a stronghold of feudalism cheek by jowl
with the quiet mansion of a colonial gentleman.
There Touraine jostles Constantinople ; and the
climax is reached by Mr Schwab, who has decreed
for himself a lofty pleasure-dome, which is said to
resemble Chambord, and which takes its place in a
long line of villas, without so much as a turnip-field

to give it an air of seclusion or security. In this vain-glorious craving for discomfort there is a kind of *naïveté* which is not without its pathos. One proud lady, whose husband, in the words of a dithyrambic guide-book, " made a fortune from a patent glove-hook," boasts that her mansion has a glass-room on the second floor. Another vain householder deems it sufficient to proclaim that he spent two million dollars upon the villa which shelters him from the storm. In brief, there is scarcely a single palace on the Riverside which may not be described as an antic of wealth, and one wonders what sort of a life is lived within these gloomy walls. Do the inhabitants dress their parts with conscientious gravity, and sit down to dine with the trappings of costume and furniture which belong to their houses ? Suppose they did, and suppose in obedience to a signal they precipi-tated themselves upon the highway, there would be such a masquerade of fancy dress as the world has never seen.

The Riverside Drive, then, is a sermon in stones, whose text is the uselessness of uncultured dollars. If we judged New York by this orgie of tasteless extravagance, we might condemn it for a *parvenu* among cities, careless of millions and sparing of discretion. We may not thus judge it. New York, if it be a *parvenu*, is often a *parvenu* of taste, and has given many a proof of intelligence and refinement. The home of great luxury, it does not always, as on the Riverside, mistake display for beauty. There are houses in the neighbourhood of Fifth Avenue which are perfect in reticence and suitability. The clubs of New York are a splendid example even to London, the first home of clubs. In Central Park the people of New York possesses a place of amenity and recreation which Europe cannot surpass ; and when you are tired of watching the antics of the leisurely chipmunk, who gambols without haste and without fear, you may delight in a collection of pictures which wealth and good management will make the despair and admiration of the world. Much, of course, remains to do, and therein New York is fortunate. Her growing interest in sculpture and architecture is matched by a magnificent opportunity. In the Old World all has been accomplished. Our buildings are set up, our memorials dedicated, our pictures gathered into galleries. America starts, so to say, from scratch ; there is no limit to her ambition ; and she has infinite money. If the past is ours, the future is hers, and we may look forward to it with curiosity and with hope.

The architects of America have not only composed works in accordance with the old traditions and in obedience to ancient models ; they have devised a new style and a new method of their own. To pack a vast metropolis within a narrow space, they have made mountains of houses. When the rock upon which their city stands proved insufficient for their ambition, they conquered another kingdom in the air. The sky-scrapers which lift their lofty turrets to the heavens are the pride of New York. It is upon them that the returning traveller gazes most eagerly, as he nears the shore. They hold a firmer place in his heart than even the statue of Liberty, and the vague sentiment which it inspires. With a proper vanity he points out to the poor Briton, who shudders at five storeys, the size and grandeur of his imposing palaces. And his arrogance is just. The sky-scraper presents a new view of architecture. It is original, characteristic, and beautiful. Suggested and enforced, as I have said, by the narrowness of the rock, it is suitable to its atmosphere and environment. New York is a southern, sunlit city, which needs protection from the heat and need not fear obscurity. Even where the buildings are highest, the wayfarer does not feel that he is walking at the bottom of a well. But, let it be said at once, the sky-scraper would be intolerable in our grey and murky land. London demands a broad thoroughfare and low houses. These are its only defence against a covered sky and an enveloping fog, and the patriotic Americans who would transplant their sky-scrapers to England merely prove that they do not appreciate the logic and beauty of their own design.

What, then, is a sky-scraper? It is a giant bird-cage, whose interstices are filled with stone or concrete. Though its structure is concealed from the eye, it is impossible not to wonder at its superb effrontery. It depends for its effect, not upon ornament, which perforce appears trivial and inapposite, but upon its mass. Whatever approaches it of another scale and kind is dwarfed to insignificance. The Sub-Treasury of the United States, for instance, looks like a foolish plaything beside its august neighbours. Where sky-scrapers are there must be no commemorative statues, no monuments raised to merely human heroes. The effigy of Washington in Wall Street has no more dignity than a tin soldier. And as the sky-scraper makes houses of a common size ridiculous, so it loses its splendour when it stands alone. Nothing can surpass in ugliness the twenty storeys of thin horror that is called the Flat-iron ; and it is ugly because it is isolated in Madison Square, a place of reasonable dimensions. It is continuity which imparts a dignity to these mammoths. The vast masses which frown upon Wall Street and Broadway are austere, like the Pyramids. They seem the works of giants, not of men. They might be a vast phenomenon of nature, which was before the flood, and which has survived the shocks of earthquake and the passage of the years. And when their summits are lit by the declining sun, when their white walls look like marble in the glow of the reddening sky, they present such a spectacle as many a strenuous American crosses the ocean to see in Switzerland, and crosses it in vain.

New York in truth, is a city of many beauties, and with a reckless prodigality she has done her best to obscure them all. Driven by a vain love of swift traffic, she assails your ear with an incessant din and your eye with the unsightliest railroad that human ingenuity has ever contrived. She has sacrificed the amenity of her streets and the dignity of her buildings to the false god of Speed. Why men worship Speed, a demon who lies in wait to destroy them, it is impossible to understand. It would be as wise and as profitable to worship Sloth. However, the men of New York, as they tell you with an insistent and ingenious pride, are 'hustlers.' They must ever be moving, and moving fast. The 'hustling' probably leads to little enough. Haste and industry are not synonymous. To run up and down is but a form of busy idleness. The captains of industry who do the work of the world sit still, surrounded by bells and telephones. Such heroes as J. Pierpont Morgan and John D. Rockefeller are never surprised on train or trolley. They show themselves furtively behind vast expanses of plate-glass, and move only to eat or sleep. It is the common citizen of New York who is never quiet. He finds it irksome to stay long in the same place. Though his house may be comfortable, even luxurious, he is in a fever to leave it. And so it comes about that what he is wont to call 'transportation' seems the most important thing in his life. We give the word another signification. To New York it means the many methods of conveying passengers from one point to another. And the methods, various as they are, keep pace with the desires of the restless citizen, who may travel at what pace and altitude he desires. He may burrow, like a rabbit, beneath the ground. If he be more happily normal in his tastes he may ride in a surface car. Or he may fly, like a bird through the air, on an overhead railway. The constant rattle of cars and railways is indescribable. The overhead lines pass close to the first-floor windows, bringing darkness and noise wherever they are laid. There are offices in which a stranger can neither hear nor be heard, and yet you are told that to the accustomed ear of the native all is silent and reposeful. And I can easily believe that a sudden cessation of din would bring an instant madness. Nor must another and an indirect result of the trains and trams which encircle New York be forgotten. The roads are so seldom used that they are permitted to fall into a ruinous decay. Their surface is broken into ruts and yawns in chasms. To drive 'down-town' in a carriage is to suffer a sensation akin to sea-sickness; and having once suffered, you can understand that it is something else than the democratic love of travelling in common that persuades the people of New York to clamber on the overhead railway, or to take its chance in a tram-car.

Movement, then, noisy and incessant, is the passion of New York. Perhaps it is the brisk air which drives men to this useless activity. Perhaps it is no better than an ingrained and superstitious habit. But the drowsiest foreigner is soon caught up in the whirl. He needs neither rest nor sleep. He too must be chasing something which always eludes him. He too finds himself leaving a quiet corner where he would like to stay, that he may reach some place which he has no desire to see. Even though he mount to the tenth or the twentieth storey, the throb of the restless city reaches him. Wall Street is ' hustling ' made concrete. The Bowery is crowded with a cosmopolitan horde which is never still. Brooklyn Bridge and Brooklyn Ferry might be the crossroads of the world. There a vast mob is passing hither and thither, on foot, on boats, on railroads. What are they doing, whither are they going, these scurrying men and women ? Have they no business to pursue, no office-stool to sit upon, no typewriting machines to jostle ? And when you are weary of ' transportation,' go into the hall of a big hotel, and you will find the same ceaseless motion. On all sides you will hear the *click, click,* of telephone and telegram. On all sides you will see eager citizens scanning the tape, which brings them messages of ruin or success. Nowhere, save in a secluded bar or a stately club, will you find a single man content to be alive and to squander the leisure that God has given him.

And with all her undying haste New York is not content. She must still find other means of saving time. And to save time she has strained all the resources of civilization. In that rather dismal thing called ' material progress ' she is easily ahead of the world. Never was the apparatus of life so skilfully turned and handled as in New York. There are no two fixed points which are not easily connected by iron lines. There seems no reason why a citizen of

New York should ever walk. If stairs exist, he need not use them, for an express lift, warranted not to stop before the fifteenth floor, will carry him in a few seconds to the top of the highest building. If he open a cupboard door, the mere opening of it lights an electric lamp, and he need not grope after a coat by the dim light of a guttering candle. At his bed-head stands a telephone, and, if he will, he may speak to a friend a thousand miles away without moving from his pillow. But time is saved—of that there is no doubt. The only doubt is, whether it be worth saving. When New York has saved her time, what does she do with it? She merely squanders it in riotous movement and reckless 'transportation.' Thus she lives in a vicious circle—saving time that she may spend it, and spending it that again she may save it. Nor can this material progress be achieved without a loss of what the Old World prizes most highly. To win all the benefits which civilization affords, you must lose peace and you must sacrifice privacy. The many appliances which save our useless time may be enjoyed only by crowds. The citizens of New York travel, live, and talk in public. They have made their choice, and are proud of it. Englishmen are still reckless enough to waste their time in pursuit of individualism, and I think they are wise. For my part, I would rather lose my time than save it, and the one open conveyance of New York which in pace and conduct suits my inclination is the Fifth Avenue Stage.

But New York is unique. It baffles the understanding and defies observation. In vain you search for a standard of comparison. France and England set out many centuries ago from the same point and with the same intention. America has nothing in common, either of purpose or method, with either of these countries. To a European it is the most foreign city on earth. Untidy but flamboyant, it is reckless of the laws by which life is lived elsewhere. It builds beautiful houses, it delights in white marble palaces, and it thinks it superfluous to level its roads. Eager for success, worshipping astuteness as devoutly as it worships speed, it is yet indifferent to the failure of others, and seems to hold human life in light esteem. In brief, it is a braggart city of medieval courage and medieval cruelty, combining the fierceness of an Italian republic with a perfect faith in mechanical contrivance and an ardent love of material progress.

Here, then, are all the elements of interest and curiosity. Happy are the citizens who watch from day to day the fight that never before has been fought on the same terms. And yet more strangely baffling than the city are the citizens. Who are they, and of what blood and character? What, indeed, is a New Yorker? Is he Jew or Irish? Is he English or German? Is he Russian or Polish? He may be something of all these, and yet he is wholly none of them. Something has been added to him which he had not before. He is endowed with a briskness and an invention often alien to his blood. He is quicker in his movement, less trammelled in his judgments. Though he may lose wisdom in sharpening his wit, the change he undergoes is unmistakable. New York, indeed, resembles a magic cauldron. Those who are cast into it are born again. For a generation some vague trace of accent or habit may remain. The old characteristics must needs hang about the newly arrived immigrant. But in a generation these characteristics are softened or disappear, and there is produced a type which seems remote from all its origins.

As yet the process of amalgamation is incomplete, and it is impossible to say in what this hubble-shubble of mixed races will result. Nor have we any clue of historical experience which we may follow. The Roman Empire included within its borders many lands and unnumbered nationalities, but the dominant race kept its blood pure. In New York and the other great cities of America the soil is the sole common factor. Though all the citizens of the great republic live upon that soil, they differ in blood and origin as much as the East of Europe differs from the West. And it is a mystery yet unpierced that, as the generations pass, they approach nearer and nearer to uniformity, both in type and character.

And by what traits do we recognize the citizen of New York? Of course there is no question here of the cultivated gentleman, who is familiar in Paris and London, and whose hospitality in his own land is an amiable reproach to our own too frequent thoughtlessness, but of the simpler class which confronts the traveller in street and train, in hotel and restaurant. The railway guard, the waiter, the cab-driver—these are the men upon whose care the comfort of the stranger depends in every land, and whose tact and temper are no bad index of the national character. In New York, then, you are met everywhere by a sort of urbane familiarity. The man who does you a service, for which you pay him, is neither civil nor uncivil. He contrives, in a way which is by no means unpleasant, to put himself on an equality with you. With a mild surprise you find yourself taking for granted what in your own land you would resent bitterly. Not even the curiosity of the nigger, who brushes your coat with a whisk, appears irksome. For the habit of years has enabled white man and black to assume a light and easy manner, which in an Englishman, born and trained to another tradition, would appear impertinence.

And familiarity is not the only trait which separates the plain man of New York from the plain man of London. The New Yorker looks upon the foreigner with the eye of patronage. To his superior intelligence the wandering stranger is a kind of natural, who should not be allowed to roam alone and at large. Before you have been long in the land you find yourself shepherded, and driven with an affability, not unmixed with contempt, into the right path. Again, you do not resent it, and yet are surprised at your own forbearance. A little thought, however, explains the assumed superiority. The citizen of New York has an ingenuous pride and pleasure in his own city and in his own prowess, which nothing can daunt. He is convinced, especially if he has never travelled beyond his own borders, that he engrosses the virtue and intelligence of the world. The driver of a motor-car assured me, with a quiet certitude which brooked no contradiction, that England was cut up into sporting estates for the "lords," and that there the working man was doomed to an idle servility. "But," said he, "there is no room for bums here." This absolute disbelief in other countries, combined with a perfect confidence in their own, has persuaded the citizens of New York to look down with a cold and pitiful eye upon those who are so unfortunate as to be born under an effete monarchy. There is no bluster in their attitude, no insistence. The conviction of superiority is far too great for that. They belong to the greatest country upon earth ; they alone enjoy the true blessings of freedom ; they alone understand the dignity of labour

F

and the spirit of independence ; and they have made up their minds kindly but firmly that you shall not forget it.

Thus you carry away from New York a memory of a lively air, gigantic buildings, incessant movement, sporadic elegance, and ingenuous patronage. And when you have separated your impressions, the most vivid and constant impression that remains is of a city where the means of life conquer life itself, whose citizens die hourly of the rage to live.

From "American Sketches"

THE SHOPS AND TAVERNS
OF PICCADILLY

G. S. STREET

THE prejudice against trade is quite a modern sort of snobbishness. Down to the eighteenth century—and there are later instances still—it was common for country gentlemen to apprentice their younger sons to tradesmen in the nearest town, and every one knows that the City merchants of old days were very often men of ancient family and gentle breeding. When there was a Court party in bitter opposition to the City party, the prejudice had some natural and excusable reason in it; nowadays, I imagine, its chief motive force is the desire of people, in our tiresome and incessant social scramble, to make the most of their own advantage by insisting on a social disability in others, and it exposes its meanness and futility by ceasing immediately when the trading is on a large scale. Happily, it is nearly dead among the intelligent, but its stupidity annoys me, and I am sorry, therefore, that I cannot help to slay it, in my remarks on the old shops of Piccadilly, by pointing to a number of bygone tradesmen with beautiful, or at any rate interesting, qualities. Alas! I cannot. Men who build up and run successful businesses have intelligence and strength of character, and most often prudence and temperance. But these are cold virtues, not striking or picturesque. Their useful lives are necessarily a little humdrum or so.

Nothing very passionate or romantic is likely to be recorded of them. So one falls back on the characters of the shops, which, of course, may have an individuality of their own, partly made up of association with famous customers. Their present functions— where they still exist—are of course beside my theme, but they have ghostly memories.

Among the shops of Piccadilly, booksellers have been from very early days honourably prominent. There was Wright's at 169, for example, where the *Anti-Jacobin* was published, and where, indeed, the editors laboured on the first floor. I fear that few of my readers, to whom this is news, are likely to go and gaze reverently on the building. Social satire, when it is really good, is more or less for all time, but political satire dies. We all know " The Needy Knife-grinder," but how many of us know anything else which appeared in the *Anti-Jacobin* ? However, George Canning was greater than the paper he inspired, and Wright's shop (as Hatchard's a little later) must have known him well. He lived, for a while, nearly opposite, in the Albany, and must have been a familiar figure crossing Piccadilly.

In and outside Wright's shop there took place a famous row—one might have had a separate chapter on the rows of Piccadilly. A violent row, but not on a great scale, like Sir Francis Burdett's, or a romantic attempt at murder, like Blood's on the Duke of Ormonde, or even a gentlemanly row, like my Lords Bath and Hervey's duel just inside the Green Park ; only one of those unseemly scuffles which were all that literary men—in past ages, of course, I mean— were generally able to accomplish. Gifford was a great critic and editor, as you know, and Wolcot, known as " Peter Pindar," was also a great critic, and

they hated one another. Gifford wrote an *Epistle to
Peter Pindar*, in which he remarked that

> Thou canst not think, nor have I power to tell
> How much I scorn and loathe thee—so farewell.

It was rather a boyish insult, and I can lay my
hand on my heart and say that if anyone said it to
me I should laugh. Wolcot, however, was furious,
and waited for Gifford outside Wright's, and rushing
after him into the shop gave him one on the nob with
a stick. But Gifford, who in boyhood had used his
hands at sea, and in a bootmaker's shop, was too
strong for Wolcot, and rolled him into the gutter.
I hope he did it without assistance, but there is a
regrettable mention of a bystander seizing Wolcot's
arm. He was really very silly to mind Gifford's
loathing him.

No such painful scene ever troubled the peace of
Hatchard's, which was originally hard by, at 173.
For my knowledge of this famous shop's history, I am
indebted to an interesting book about it written by
Mr Arthur Humphreys, who does well to be proud
that the business over which he presides has such a
long and full tradition. Of the original Hatchard,
however, who had his training as a bookseller with
the celebrated Tom Payne, and set up for himself at
173 in 1797, paying £31 10s. for the goodwill, and
£40 rent, I do not find much to repeat. In fact, I
think the most interesting thing Mr Humphreys gives
us about the man himself is a detailed description of
his dress, for that allows us to picture him accurately
as he moved among his customers. " He was invariably dressed in black. His coat was of the style
of a Bishop's frock-coat, waistcoat buttoning to the
throat with an entirely plain front, and knee-breeches

and gaiters." A most respectable figure indeed.
He did a thriving business in pamphlets, publishing,
in the very first year, one which was an immense
success, to wit, *Reform or Ruin : Take your Choice !*
which appears to have been a spirit-exhortation to
respectability, and was written by no less a person
than John Bowdler, father of the more notorious
Thomas. Hatchard moved to 190 in 1801, and later
to 187, where the business now is. The political
pamphlets were in the Tory interest, and the people
who frequented Hatchard's to loaf and gossip there
in the pleasant fashion of that day, were mostly on
the Tory side. Sydney Smith glanced at them with
unkind humour in an *Edinburgh Review* article in 1810.
" There is a set of well-dressed, prosperous gentlemen
who assemble daily at Mr Hatchard's shop, clean,
civil personages, well in with the people in power,
delighted with every existing institution, and almost
with every existing circumstance, and every now and
then one of these personages writes a little book, and
the rest praise that little book, expecting to be praised
in their turn for their own little books, and of
these little books thus written by these clean, civil
personages so expecting to be praised, the pamphlet
before us appears to be one." We have heard of
such societies, mutually helpful in the book-pushing
way, since that date—equally clean and civil, let us
hope.

Hatchard's was also the rendezvous of societies
more formally constituted. The Royal Horticul-
tural Society was formed there, and so was a much
more amusing society called the Outinian. This
was a body for the promotion of marriages, an object
it was to attain by the dubious process of inquiring
into the suitability of the contracting parties and

supplying helpful information to members who intended to marry. It began its meetings by the consumption of tea and buns. John Hatchard, it appears, lent his initials as well as his premises to this agreeable little institution, and Mr Humphreys wonders how he could have mixed himself up in so absurd an affair. I hope I may suggest, without disrespect to the notoriously altruistic nature of publishers, that John charged something. As for the appearance of Hatchard's when the clean and civil personages and the Outinians met there, it was much as it is now, with a bench outside for servants, a fireplace—those features restored by Mr Humphreys —a table with the daily papers on it, and chairs for the weary and sleepy. It was lit, of course, by oil lamps. One may imagine all sorts of celebrities buying books at Hatchard's ; of those more particularly associated with it were Macaulay, who used to be sent in his youth to buy books there by Hannah More ; Hannah herself, who longed as a girl " to go to London to see Bishops and booksellers," and William Wilberforce.

Booksellers, like brave men, need a bard if their memories are to live, and it is thanks to Mr Humphreys that I have lingered over Hatchard's. But there are others who at least must be mentioned. Ridgway's was already established when Hatchard went to Piccadilly. Almon, opposite Burlington House also, was gone, succeeded by Debrett, who had been in partnership with him. A *Letter to Edmund Burke* in 1782 refers pleasantly to " that common sink of filth and fiction, the shop of Almon and Debrett in Piccadilly." The reason of this description was that Almon's, a great Whig firm, had published the *Letters in Favour of Wilkes*, etc., in 1764.

I wish we had still those political antagonisms in shops.

A shop which has followed Mr Humphrey's good example and published an account of itself, is that of Fortnum and Mason—ministering to the body as Hatchard's to the mind. " A. M. B." has written an informing little brochure, with interesting pictures, about Piccadilly and this ancient house of good things to eat. It beats Hatchard's, indeed, in point of antiquity, for the business was started, appropriately, in the days of Queen Anne, who, as we know, liked tea—and things to eat and drink generally—and it has been in Piccadilly for a hundred and fifty years. Stewart's too, the confectioner's at the corner of Bond Street, is an ancient affair. But I want a hero, as Byron says, or at least a character. . . . " I'll therefore take our ancient friend " Hoby, the boot-maker, who was deservedly thought a character in his day. My seeming irrelevant quotation was in fact a subconscious inspiration, for there is a reference to Hoby in one of Byron's letters. It was in 1820, at the time of Queen Caroline's trial, and Byron writes : " I hear Mr Hoby says that it makes him weep to see her—she reminded him so much of Jane Shore." Jane Shore was a popularly pathetic part in the theatre of the time, but certainly it was not a happy simile for Hoby to make, and Byron wrote a verse on it :

> Mr Hoby the Bootmaker's soft heart is sore,
> For seeing the Queen makes him think of Jane Shore,
> And in fact . . .

He has two lines more, but in another letter he omits them, and so will I, on the whole. Hoby was in business at 160 Piccadilly in 1808, as an advertise-ment in *The Stranger's Guide to London* of that date informs us. He was a humorist, Hoby, as well as a man of sentiment. When a dissatisfied young ensign threatened to leave him, he turned to his shopman with an order to put up the shutters, for that all was over, he was a ruined man. A king among boot-makers was Hoby. To discourse much further of shops might bring me too near to writing a stranger's guide to London of my own. But I must not forgo a compliment to Lincoln Bennett's hat-shop, for the distinction of standing where stood the house of Sir William Petty, founder of the Lansdowne family, and friend of Samuel Pepys.

One might think in one's haste that taverns would make a livelier subject, but the thoughtful reader is aware that few reflections are more melancholy than those suggested by long-gone feasting and drinking. It is sadder to think that those who laughed, than that those who wept, are dead. Happily, however, the local associations of good cheer have a way of persisting. The White Bear Inn, for example, had a history of nigh two hundred years before it disappeared, and the Criterion restaurant keeps up the general association on its site. The White Bear had memories of art about it. Benjamin West lay there when he arrived from America, and Luke Sullivan, who engraved Hogarth's *March to Finchley*, died there. So died another engraver, one Chatelain, in 1771. He had in excess what I suppose the enemies of artists mean by the artistic temperament. He engraved for Mr Toms, who paid him a shilling an hour ; having worked for half an hour, he would demand his sixpence, and spend it forthwith in drink. As Mr Wheatley says, this was a very improvident man. *Deus sit propitius*. . . . It was fitting he should die in a tavern. There was a Black Bear as well as a

White Bear at this end of Piccadilly. The black rival was nearly opposite until 1820 ; not knowing its exact site, I am fain to hope some restaurant or other stands on it.

There is no such doubt about the Gloster Coffee-house and Hotel, for that was at the corner of Berkeley Street, where is now the Berkeley, sometime called the St James's Hotel. The Gloster was a very old house, and I find it flourishing in 1805, when a dear little book, called *The Picture of London*, advertises it as supplying " good soups, dinners, wines, and beds." The soup suggests a warm refreshment before starting by coach in the morning, and of course these Piccadilly inns were famous for coaching connexions. There was the Three Kings at No. 67, whence General Palmer started the first mail-coach to Bath, and where stands the present Hatchett's. There was the Old White Horse Cellar at 155 ; the Ritz now occupies that site. It is mentioned by Strype in 1720, and my *Picture of London* tells us that " this house is well known to the public on account of the great number of stage-coaches which regularly call there. In a pleasant coffee-room passengers can wait for any of the stages, and travellers in general are well accommodated with beds." One imagines, of course, a great deal of bustle in these taverns and coffee-houses of old : it has been called to life in books often enough. The English, it is said—and truly, I think—have grown more reserved in manner, and certainly have grown more to a pattern. One must imagine many more eccentrics, much more shouting and advice and protest and argument than one can hear now at a railway-station, more variety and colour of dress too, and altogether a livelier and gayer scene.

While we are imagining, too, we must not forget the commonplace that the taverns were crowded with folk well acquainted with one another and talking intimately together, who now would go to clubs. That is still to some extent the case with the ' lower classes,' but with no others. Even Bohemia has left the tavern for the club, although I have known more than one public-house where artists of one sort or another were to be regularly found. Certainly no Squire Western of to-day, coming to London, would drink and collogue with the landlord of an inn, as Fielding's Squire Western did with him of The Hercules Pillars. That famous inn was at Hyde Park Corner, and stood there as late as 1797, being mentioned as early (by Wycherley, in his *Plain Dealer*) as 1676. The great Marquis of Granby, who gave his name to so many other inns, used to frequent it ; and Sheridan and Captain Mathews went there when they were interrupted in their duel about the melodious Miss Linley. There was many another tavern at Hyde Park Corner—a Red Lion and a Golden Lion, and so forth—and, by the way, at the beginning of the eighteenth century, a place called Winstanley's Water Theatre, where mechanical contrivances astonished our simple ancestors. It advertised as its great attraction—in a *Guardian* of 1713— "6 sorts of wine and brandy, to drink the Queen's health, all coming out of the barrel, with bisket and spaw water ; and, as peace is inlarged, there will be added Claret, Pale Ale, Stout and Water playing out of the head of the barrel when it is in the pulley." The ingenious Henry Winstanley, among other devices in his house at Littlebury, had one passing strange. If a visitor (so it is said) kicked an old slipper lying on the floor, a ghost started up before him. Winstanley's ghost, if it walks, must pass from the scene of his entertainment at Hyde Park Corner up Piccadilly to the site of the Egyptian Hall, and muse over conjuring improvements. Man and his marvels pass away, and it is not strange that Water Theatre and Egyptian Hall should be gone. But it does seem odd that of the eight, or so, public-houses at Hyde Park Corner, not one remains. The fact must sadden many a ghostly toper.

From " The Ghosts of Piccadilly "

SUNSET FROM THE GATE OF BAIDARI

STEPHEN GRAHAM

IT was at the Gate of Baidari in the Crimea on the shortest day of the year that I saw the most wonderful sunset I have ever known, and entered most completely into the spirit of the dark, quiet night.

It was another vision of the sea, a presentment of the sea's question in a new light.

A mild December afternoon. I had been some days wandering across pleasant tree-brown valleys and immense hollows mountain-walled. In the winter silence there was no murmur of the ocean, not even was there saltness in the air. I was out of the sight of the sea and had been so for several days. But this afternoon I climbed by a long road where were many berberry-bushes vermilion with their berries, up to the pass over the hills, and there all at once by surprise, without the least expecting it, at a turn of the road I had a revelation of the whole sea.

It was a ravishment of the eyes, a scene on which one looks, at which one stares. The road came suddenly to a precipice, and sheer down, two thousand feet below, the waves foamed forward on the rocks, and from the foam to the remote horizon lay the mysterious sleeping sea—no, not sleeping, but rather causing all else to sleep in its presence, for it was full of serpent lines all moving toward the shore. The whole wild mountainous Crimean shore sat before the sea and dreamed.

And I realized slowly all that was in the evening. Below me lay the white tortuous road leading downward to the shore in coils, and clothing the road, the many woods, all hoary white because the sharp seabreeze had breathed on them. Evening had long since settled on the road and on the wintry trees ; it lay also about the grey temple which the Russians have put up on one of the platforms of the lower cliffs. The church looked so compact and small down below me that it seemed one could have held it in the palm of the hand. It was sunset, but the sky was full of blue-grey colour. The whole south caught a radiance from the hidden west and the sea was grey.

In a moment it is noticeable that the south is becoming rosier. The sea is now alight from the increase of sunset hues. In the shadow the lines of the sea are a sequence of wavings like the smoke of the snow blown over the steppes. In the hurrying clouds a great space clears, and along the south-west runs a great rosy fleece of sunset. It is rapidly darkening. The sea in the western corner is crimson, but all the vast south is silver and sombre. The horizon is like that seen from a balloon—pushed out to its furthermost, and there, where clouds and sky mingle, one sees fantastically as it were the sides of giant, shadowy fish.

The motor-coach, with its passengers from Sebastopol to Yalta, comes rushing and grumbling up behind me and stops five minutes, this being its half-way point. The passengers adjourn into the inn to drink vodka : " Remember, gentlemen, five minutes only," says the chauffeur. " God help anyone who gets left behind at Baidari. . . ." Four minutes later there is a stamping of fat men in heavy overcoats round the brightly varnished bus. " Are we going? " says a little man to the refreshed but purple-faced chauffeur. " Yes ! " " That's good. I've had enough of this." The guard winds his horn, and after a preliminary squirm of the plump tyres on the soft road the vehicle and its company goes tumbling down the road as if it were descending into a pit.

And the sunset ! It develops with every instant. The lines on the sea seem to move more quickly, and the spaces between them to be larger. The west is full of storm. A closing cloud comes up out of the west : the western sea is utterly hopeless, the moving south inexorable. There is terror in the west.

Evening is more below me than above me. Night is coming to me over the dark woods. The foam on the rocks below is like a milk-white robe. As I walk the first miles downhill I begin to hear the sound of the waves. The sea is beginning to roar, and the wind rushing up to me tells me that the lines of the sea are its stormy waves ridden forward to the shore by a gale.

I stood on the platform where the many-domed temple was built, and watched the gathering night. Unnumbered trees lay beneath me, but it was so dusk I hardly knew them to be trees. The gigantic black cliff that shuts off the west stood blank into the heaven like a great door : to the east lay the ghostly fading coast-line of Aloopka. Among the black clouds overhead danced out happy fires, and, answering their brightness, windows lighted up in cottages far below, and lanterns gleamed on a little steamer just puffing over the horizon.

There came the pure December evening with frost and Christmas bells, and happy hearths somewhere in the background. The one star in the sky was a beckoning one : my heart yearned.

I dipped down upon the road, and in a few minutes was looking at the temple from below, seeing it entirely silhouetted against the sky. It was now indeed held up in a giant's palm and looked at.

Far out at sea now lay a silver strand ; the lines of the waves were all curves and heavily laden with shadows —they were, indeed, waves. Far above me the cliffs that I had left were mist-hidden, and in the midst shone a strange light from the last glow of sunset in the unseen west.

Night. At a word the sea became lineless and shapeless. The sunset sky was green-blue, and black strips of cloud lay athwart it. Looking up to the crags above me, I missed the church ; it was in heaven or in the clouds. A great wind blew, and ceased, and came no more—the one gust that I felt of a whole day's storm on the coast. Night chose to be calm, and though all the waves called in chorus upon the rocks, there was a silence and a peace within the evening that is beyond all words.

I walked with the night. I walked to find an inn, and yet cared not that the way was far and that men dwelt not in these parts. For something had entered into me from Nature, and I had lived an extra life after the day was done. It was not one person alone that, pack on back, walked that dark and quiet Crimean road. And the new spirit that was with me whispered promises and lingered over secrets half revealed. I came to know that I should really enter into it, and be one with it, that I should be part of a description of night and part of night itself.

of devilish glee, as one who says, " Well, I killed my enemy, anyway, first."

I could have watched the place for hours and days and months. Captain Webb tried to swim it. I cannot think why he was allowed to try. A wave just picked him up and squeezed him against another wave and killed him dead, as he must have seen would happen. No human being could live in such water. It has force enough to light the world and grind the world's bread beside.

From "Recent Prose"

ROUND ETNA

OSBERT SITWELL

CATANIA is, without doubt, a city to visit—but not to stay in. When once you have seen it, and, in spite of the noise and obvious squalor, have felt its attraction, moments arrive in your life when you feel compelled to return there ; but never allow yourself to be tempted to remain in the city. There is a quality of horror about these large, hot, draughty, dirty, empty, noisy hotels that is lacking in far dirtier and more palpably unpleasant ones.

Used as I am to the thoughtfulness of Southern Italian and Sicilian hotel-keepers, the dead rat deposited, apparently as a tribute, on the mat by my bedroom door, was more than I could for long endure. There it was, laid out in state, under the high glass roof of the corridor, in all its funeral pomp ; and as, bolted within my room, I lay awake, haunted by thoughts of the silent sentinel outside, the unwelcome memory of many old acquaintances in the insect, reptile, and rodent world came back to me. There were the rats in the trenches—plump brutes that dropped from the branches of shattered trees into the muddy pools below with a fat sound of splashing, as they weltered and wallowed in the mud. There were, too, those beetles in the dining-room of the small inn at Monte Cassino, where we were once stranded for the night, unable to obtain accommo-

dation at the monastery because so many dignitaries
of the Church were then making their Easter retreat
—beetles that at the slightest movement dropped in
showers from wall and curtain on to the tables and
floor below. Even worse was the recollection of my
tent in the camp at Marlowe. Situated in a large,
flat, grass field on the top of a hill, bounded by hanging wood, no English scene could have been more
beautiful, more typical of its county ; but a plague
of earwigs, perhaps the most horrible of English pests,
hung over us like a cloud, and at night, if the canvas
were ever so slightly touched, would fall squirming
on to bed and floor. There was that earwig which
had attacked me in my bath at Weston. Suddenly
looking round, I saw it parting the waters with a
vigorous side-stroke, and making for my big toe. A
terrific and lengthy battle ensued. Then there was
my old friend the scorpion, who waxes fat on the
bones of saints and holy men in the chapel at
Montegufoni. Scorpions are not common in Tuscany,
but this one has thrived for many years, possibly
protected by the patron saint upon whom he feeds.
A horrid dragon he is, as he crouches on the wall,
guarding the numerous cases of glass and gilded wood,
in which lie revealed the parchment-coloured relics,
tied up with coquettish bows of salmon-pink ribbon,
with an occasional orange-flower placed here and
there, to awaken in these dry, meagre bones memories
of the flesh that once adhered to them, but yet a
guardian preferable to that one now sleeping his last
sleep without. Finally I thought again of the snake,
which I saw on a fine August morning, clambering
up the garden-steps of the hotel where I am now
writing into what, considering the discomfort of the
chairs that grace it, is somewhat euphemistically

known as " the lounge." This snake was very impressive, not very large, but a dowager obviously,
and boasting of I know not how many quarterings ;
so heraldic, so viperous was it, that anywhere it would
have passed as the model for the Sforza coat-of-arms ;
and the Sforzas, in truth, sprang from the same soil.
" Only something come in from the lake," the porter
reassured me, as he disposed of its mangled corpse ;
but I have never yet met reptile or insect that failed
to rouse my loathing, and I lay in bed praying for the
day of Wells' Utopia, when none of such things would
be permitted to exist, except as caged specimens of
the evils that men had for many millions of years
borne willingly, making no concerted effort to destroy, content with attempting the extermination of
their own kind.

Alas, even a dead rat may affect human happiness
more than one would, at first, deem possible. In
order to avoid other encounters of this kind I decided
to move on, ten miles or so, to Acireale. Here, it
was stated, was a new and comfortable hotel in a
little-frequented city on the beautiful slopes of Etna.
As a matter of strict accuracy, the hotel was an old
one, that for some reason or other had remained
empty for twenty years, but its renovation was sufficiently recent for the paint on the wall to be still
damp, and the rooms quite unheated. January
nights are cold everywhere, even in Sicily, and as a
result I caught a chill and influenza, and was ill for
some time.

That hotel, an immense building on the highroad,
near the railway, will ever remain a mystery. If you
sleep on the side of the street, the passing railway
engine almost puts its funnel in at your window and
runs under the bed ; on the other side is a gloomy

but rather beautiful view of Etna. The bedrooms are few—about thirty—but lofty. The bathrooms are many, but with no hope of water. The sitting-rooms are of immense size ; the dining-room, with its high, vaulted ceiling, is a really beautiful room, large enough to seat four or five hundred people. Its actual owner was an immensely rich and eccentric Sicilian nobleman, who paid for everything, and it was run by a charming, fat Sicilian hotel-keeper. But were this hotel everything that was promised of it, who except an occasional visitor like myself would wish to stay in—or come to—such a town ? . . . We were promised orange-groves, gardens of deliciously smelling flowers, constant hot water, shower-baths, an American bar, two tennis-courts ; . . . but all these things were but mirages, the figments of the Sicilian Marchese's fervent imagination, the product of my fat friend's realistic literary style. For the non-existence of the tennis-courts we were, however, duly grateful, because those people who come to the slopes of Etna from England and America in order to play tennis or golf must be very unpleasant mental de-fectives, and ones, too, who usually evince a passion for general conversation.

There was on this occasion little danger of casual conversation, since we were the first and only guests in the establishment. Being therefore regarded as somewhat in the nature of mascots, we were invited by our genial manager to attend the opening cere-mony of his new hotel, which was to be blessed publicly by the Bishop of Acireale at three o'clock the following afternoon. The host, I regret to write, did not altogether believe in the efficacy of this bene-diction, but he told me that the people of the town —a city of sixty thousand souls, full of the prosperous

and well educated as well as of poor illiterates—were
so deeply religious that, unless the hotel received the
episcopal blessing, not one of them would enter its
doors.

A crowd of managers, secretaries, and local mag-
nates, all clad solemnly in frock-coats, was waiting
in the hall, when punctually at two-fifty-five a motor-
car (provided by the hotel) drew up at the door.
Its large panes of glass revealed the Bishop within,
in the full glory of robes, mitre, and crook. Immediately the crowd dashed to the door, each member
of it hoping to be the first to kiss the ring. The
ceremony then began, about four hundred guests
being present. The Bishop, a very solemn figure,
walked slowly, followed by the crowd, through the
corridors, bedrooms, and high, vaulted sitting-rooms,
while an acolyte in front scattered holy water, or
occasionally himself would lift two fingers in the
gesture of benediction. We then all hurried downstairs to the dining-room, to engage in an orgy of
ices and sweet champagne, for in Sicily men—even
bishops—do not scorn an ice as they do in Northern
countries. A mandolin band, meanwhile, treated us
to selections from *Carmen* and *Rigoletto* ; but the
Bishop, in order not to spoil too much the general
enjoyment by his austere presence, soon swept out to
the strains of the march in *Aïda*—music very appropriate to him, as he strode out in his mitre, which
conjured up visions of the high-priests of Egypt. The
music now changed ; Neapolitan songs and rather
decadent ragtime became the order of the evening,
and dancing lasted for some hours.

It must be admitted that, in January, Acireale is
an unpleasant place. There is always something a
little irritating about a town that is near but not on

the sea, nor yet high enough above it, as for example
is Ravello, to make the sin of omission excusable.
Nor here has the sea receded, as at Ravenna ; so
that no extenuating circumstance can be pleaded on
behalf of its citizens, who must be a dull, unimagina-
tive body ; while, owing to the buildings and general
lay-out of the town, it is difficult even to obtain a
view of the blue waters. Worse still, the town is
situated too near Etna, the other chief feature of the
landscape, to obtain a view of it, such as you get from
places as far removed as Taormina and Syracuse,
while the smoke from the craters drifts over the town,
blotting out the sunshine that makes the days warm
even in January, causing constant showers of rain,
and giving the place temporarily the atmosphere of
Sheffield or the Five Towns. Etna is an object of
such beauty that, while so near the mountain, to be
deprived of the view of it is a real misfortune. From
Taormina it dominates the landscape absolutely, yet
has an idyllic pastoral beauty ; the long gradual
slope seems to fill the horizon, the smoke being like
a white cloud reflecting and reversing its snow-cap in
the sky above, contradicting the usual order of pool
and tree, lake and hill. From Syracuse it floats far
off, and even more beautiful, high above the flat
landscape and peacock-winged sea. From here it
seems all snow, like a large snow mound, or the icy
tent of some Arctic god, Woden or Thor, who must
have marched hither with the Northern armies. From
Catania it is more impressive, perhaps less lovely,
because its colour is black—a huge black giant, the
old Cyclops, who will soon crush the town by hurling
down on it immense rocks. But from Acireale you
can see little of it, though at night you could hear
the subterranean thunder. And at the time of which

I am writing there was a queer feeling in the air :
the great eruption which took place a few months
later was already, no doubt, being prepared below ;
and after dark, when the shrilling of the bells and
hoarse voices of the men driving their mules over the
almost impassable roads had died down, the air was
resonant with distant roaring—bellowing almost—and
Etna would be revealed crowned with such fire as had
not been seen for many decades.   We comforted ourselves by reflecting that usually while a volcano is
very active there is less danger of sudden explosion ;
but we could not help picturing the scenes if an
eruption should take place. The country lanes at
this time of year hardly exist at all, the streets and
roads of the town were as foul as those of towns in
England two hundred years ago. These would be
utterly choked and blocked by the rush of fugitives,
rough men at any time and now mad with fear, from
the slopes of Etna, one of the most thickly populated
districts in the world. They would come down in
this direction, seeking the sea as a means of escape.
They would be in a panic, have no discipline. Theft
and murder would be common among them, and the
foreigner caught in such a sudden orgy of terror
would have little chance. And all the time the red
snakes of the lava would be hissing, uncoiling down
the mountain, like huge dragons, swallowing up
whole orchards, gardens, and even towns. The only
man who would be able to stay the terror in any
degree (and dreadful his responsibility !) would be
the Bishop. The churches would be full of the
calmer part of the population kneeling to pray, re-
fusing to leave even though the roof was breaking
down under the weight of ashes. The air outside
would be hot, sultry, and full of poisonous fumes as

hell itself—such always is the way of eruptions, and such was it six months later—but in that January we thought the vision merely our evil imaginings, the result of an over-taut nervous system—just as we treated the nightmare of a world-war when it sometimes crept into our mind in the spring and early summer of 1914.

As a town Acireale is, in January at any rate, a disappointment. The opera (at which Madame Albani sang during the opening tour of her career) was not yet open. The streets were hardly possible to walk in, while to go out into the country was, obviously, an impossibility. And the whole place was dreadfully, terribly smelly. Even as regards architecture the town, though excessively strange, belied our hopes. Like most cities in the neighbourhood, it had been destroyed by the exceptionally severe earthquake of 1693. This, no doubt, overwhelmed a number of beautiful buildings here too, for nowhere else in the world are to be found so many noble examples of different styles placed near together as in Sicily. In the other parts of the island, where earthquakes are comparatively rare and mild, Greek temples, Saracenic mosques, Byzantine cathedrals, Norman castles, Gothic and Renaissance palaces, Baroque, Rococo, and Empire buildings, jostle one another in the street in a pleasing, astonishing manner. But in Acireale these relics of former civilization have either been shaken down, or lie under their coats of lava, one above the other in layers, petrified but patient, waiting for their living sister to join them, and a new one to be born in her stead.

Though this total destruction of the city must have meant the loss of most interesting monuments, it yet

gave to a town rich as this one, and in a period of
such architectural activity as was the early eighteenth
century in Sicily, a great opportunity. Think what
Wren would have done if only London had been laid
waste by earthquake as well as by fire ! But no
genius, such as his, was here to seize the chance.
Perhaps, too, there was so much building activity in
the island that no architect could be spared from,
let us say, Palermo or Syracuse. For the Rococo
creations of Palermo are particularly beautiful, re-
calling the French more than the Italian : Syracuse
is different, full of churches and palaces equal to any
of the same period, but absolutely Sicilian in style ;
while Noto, as well, is a model town of the epoch.

But when the hour for his arrival struck in Acireale,
no genius, local or foreign, appeared. On the con-
trary, far from evoking any new or appropriate style,
it seems as if the citizens, tired of earthquakes, were
eager merely to bridge over the chasms in the earth
with temporary platforms, to hide and cloak the
tremors that constantly shook the ground beneath
them with hastily improvised stages and scenery, so
as to give the pretence of a certain security and permanence to their lives. They wanted their dwellings
to have just enough of the appearance of a town to
make them feel safe from the ravages of the giant
who continually threatened them, tall enough, if
possible, to blot out his presence. They did not want
solidity, which had been proved useless, but a series
of thin-built palaces and churches, as easily put up,
as easily shaken down, as the paper houses of Japan.
On the other hand they insisted upon, at any rate,
the semblance of a background to their lives, and
were not content with mud huts and rag buildings,
as is now the population of the large city of Messina.

To give themselves this background, then, they built
their façades, and on them hung masks ; and above
these balanced wide balconies with bowlike railings.
And such masks as these were never before seen,
masks whose quality of amusement, here apparently
the only aim, was derived solely from the physical
suffering and degraded physique of a slum population;
but this trait amused each century in turn except the
nineteenth and, let us hope, the twentieth. Such
brutalized masks and debased grimaces are merely a
fantasia based upon the crowd in these cities—crowds
among which, in spite of the usually fine development
of the Sicilians, a splendid-looking race, there was
always a large proportion of dwarfs, hunchbacks, and
other monstrosities, filling the market-place with cack-
ling and idiot laughter. Yet in spite of the coarseness
of these masks and buildings, there is something impressive about them, something of the primitive
quality to be found in the totem-poles of Canada.
There is also, obviously, to be felt in them the influence of the long Spanish domination, a suggestion
of a harder people—perhaps of bull-fight and Inquisi-
tion . . . ? And this Spanish influence, while it accounts
for the air of cruelty, at the same time is the only one
that gives the buildings any artistic value, for in spite
of shortcomings, they have the vitality and strict
conventions, the rhythm and surprising dissonances
of popular Spanish music.

With the streets and squares thus hastily thrown
up, like the scenery of an improvised theatre, the life
of the town could continue as before. In the daytime an orator could address the market-place with
bold words and gestures from one of the balconies,
while the masks below reflected the democratic feelings of surprise, horror, and laughter. At night,

however, the masks would be hidden, and the balconies would become floating rafts in the air, from
which cool music could drip down into the hot ways
below, or barges, moored high among the fresh play
of the young winds, from which for once, reversing
the usual order, the ladies masked by darkness would
serenade the men waiting below, or, themselves silent,
watch the life flowing beneath them and hear the
snarling voices and deep braying of the piazzas carried
up by eddies of warm flower-scented air.

There is, however, one church that points to the
purer style and possible beauty which would have
existed in Acireale if only the earth had kept quiet
as in other lands. The church of San Sebastiano is
a noble and refined work of art. The large stone
front, with a dignity and solidity that are lightened
by the play of a whimsical and original mind, presents a great contrast to everything round it. The
wide paved platform before its portals, at the top of
a high flight of broad but shallow steps, is railed off
by a flight of Cupids, whose arms are weighed down
by the heavy chains they carry, as if to prevent the
rather brutal life of the town, mocked and sneered at
by all the leering faces that support window and
balcony, from entering to shatter the repose and peace
that are to be found within.

.   .   .   .   .   .

Before we return to our dead rat in Catania there
is one other feature of Acireale which deserves our
attention—the painted carts that go lumbering over
roads that are like a miniature model of the countryside, with rivers and hills, rocks, lakes, and precipices.
Everywhere in Sicily the peasant, when first setting
up for himself, spends an incredible proportion of his
capital—far more than he would allow himself to lay

out on the furnishing of his house or on the equipment of his farm—in buying a decorative harness and
a brightly painted cart. The harness, hung with bells
that sound, in the summer weather, cool as a splashing
shower of rain, is inset with pieces of mirror that are
for ever catching the sun's eye, tracing arabesques of
moving light on the walls of houses and gardens,
seeming indeed to echo in light the sound of the bells
in the air—for at each movement of the mule the
bells tinkle and the reflected light on the walls forms
a new design. The carts themselves vary in each
district. In Palermo, their painted panels are tra-
ditional, almost Byzantine in conception, belonging
obviously to the same world as Monreale. Of extreme brilliance in colour, they rather resemble the
Russian setting for *Coq d'Or* and *Children's Tales*, as
these were presented by M. Diaghileff. The scenes
depicted on them are usually derived from the poets.
Heroic warriors, the memory of whose chivalry and
shining armour is now only kept alive by the mario-
nette theatres, are rescuing noble but distressed
damsels. For these carts there cannot, in Palermo,
be many more than twenty patterns from among
which the peasant can choose ; going to the painter's
he *must* make his choice of one of them, since for him
to demand a new and special design would be a
breach of convention, etiquette, and almost of respectability, giving the young couple a bad name.
But the painting of the cart is not its only beauty,
for it boasts also little groups of painted wooden
statues—St George and the Dragon, and other such
subjects—as well as much fine decorative carving. In
Girgenti the carts are different, though the subjects
are identical ; they are treated less archaistically and
are in a more subdued scale of colour ; while in

H

Acireale, the peasant, here out of the hands of professional painters, and doing his own decoration, turns to modern life for his inspiration. The various panels of a cart will have portrayed on them " The Triumph of the Allies over Germany and Austria," the seizing of Fiume by d'Annunzio, a view of Etna, a toe-in-air ballerina, and an almost Derain-like still-life. But all these different types of carts, in Palermo, Girgenti, Syracuse, and here under the shadow of the volcano, are so entrancing, alive, and unself-conscious, that they probably represent the only satisfactory form of peasant-art that exists in Europe to-day.

From "Discursions on Travel, Art, and Life"

THE ART OF LIVING

ABOUT HAPPINESS

HUBERT BLAND

A GREAT and wise but much neglected philosopher once declared that "Happiness consists in following preferences."

I wonder, now, whether that strikes you as being in any sense a great and wise saying, as having any pointed application to yourself or to your scheme of life—assuming always that you have a scheme of life, an assumption which would probably be far from correct.

I don't for a moment suppose it does. I suspect, rather, that you regard it as rather a commonplace thing to have said, a sort of thing that anybody might have said, as too much of a platitude and too little of a paradox—for no doubt you have got into the bad modern habit of seeking wisdom only in paradoxes, in a kind of verbal topsy-turvydom, such as was made fashionable among the would-be intellectually *élite* in the nineties by Oscar Wilde, and which has since been rendered widely popular among the mob by Mr Bernard Shaw and his thousand and one plagiarists.

I suspect, therefore, that "Happiness consists in following preferences" is one of those dicta which you feel inclined to brush aside impatiently with an "Of course." You would have thought that philosopher to be much cleverer, much more brilliant, if he had said something like this, "Happiness consists

in being comfortably miserable," wouldn't you, now ?
That would have set you puzzling your head as to
what it could possibly mean.

It isn't " of course," you know ; it is nothing like
" of course." If it were " of course " we should all
act upon it and be happy, or, at any rate, a good
deal happier than we most of us are. To begin with,
it takes a man of average intelligence pretty well half
his life to discover with any sort of exactitude what
are his real as contrasted with his imaginary preferences, and by the time the discovery is made it is
as often as not, indeed more often than not, too late
to act upon it without revolutionizing his own life
and seriously discommoding the lives of everybody
about him.

By that time he has formed habits, habits which
were not the result of his doing what he himself liked
to do from the beginning, but of his doing what other
people liked him to do, or what he believed—quite
mistakenly, perhaps—other people thought he ought
to like to do.

Let me give an instance of the sort of thing I
mean. I have a habit—it is a habit I formed because
the practice of it pleased and amused me—when I go
to a place of public entertainment, say a theatre or
concert, of studying as narrowly as my short sight
will permit, the faces, and even the backs, of the
audiences.

Oh, I assure you, backs, when scrutinized with the
trained eye, are most expressive ; you can learn from
a back a great deal of what is going on in its owner's
mind. Men and women of the world learn how to
control their features, but rarely their backs. One
of these days I shall publish a monograph on backs
which shall replace, or at least supplement, Lavater's

masterpiece on physiognomy, and add enormously to humanity's knowledge of itself.

But to return. From a study of faces and backs at theatres and concerts I invariably divine that at least half of the persons present are wishing all the while, or at least a good part of the while, that they were somewhere else ; I perceive that they have come there, not because they wanted to come there or because they thought they would like being there when they had got there ; but because some one else wanted them to come there ; or because, for some quite inexplicable reason, they were persuaded that there was where they ought to be.

One can see quite unmistakably that they are bored stiff, these people, and that if they followed their own preferences they would get up and hurry away as fast as their own legs or a taxi-cab could carry them. But they don't ; they sit and fidget it out to the last sentence of the actor or the last note of the last cadenza.

Mention of that musical term reminds me that the obviously unwilling listener is a much more common object at concerts, or even at musical evenings, than at theatres or amateur dramatic performances. Music, I am sometimes disposed to think, is an art which doth make humbugs of us all. Observation and my penetrative insight have convinced me that at least one-half of civilized humanity actively dislikes music of every sort, and that what is called classical music it positively abhors. But not under torture would one-fiftieth part of civilized humanity admit as much—which is a most fortunate circumstance for professional musicians.

Let me give another instance of the sort of thing I mean. A night or two ago I was dining with some friends who are enthusiastic bridge players. I do not care for bridge ; rather than play it I would sit with my feet on the fender reading any old book that happened to be handy or thinking my own innocent thoughts.

But my host would not allow me to do either of those things while he and his friends were at the card-table. He declared that it would make them and him feel uncomfortable to be conscious that I was out in the cold—so he put it, though, really, I should have been in the warm, for there was an excellent fire in the room—while he and the others were enjoying themselves. Of course, I knew perfectly well that it would do nothing of the sort, that they would have forgotten my very existence after the first deal. I knew perfectly well that I should make them much more uncomfortable by playing badly, as I always do.

Nevertheless, although I was fully aware that I was doing the wrong thing, that is to say, the thing that makes for unhappiness rather than happiness, so extraordinarily difficult is it even for a philosopher to live up to his own principles that I yielded. And so, by my not acting upon the dictum that happiness consists in following preferences, five sensible men, who might have had a quite happy evening, had an evening that was not quite happy.

But you may say the principle of following your preferences may easily be carried a little too far ; that before you know where you are you may find your preferences coming into sharp conflict with those of other people, and that then there will be trouble. Further, you may say, that on the whole the thing that makes most for happiness in life is personal popularity with all with whom one comes in contact ;

and that he who makes a point of following his own preference is little likely to be popular, and so he will lose on the one hand more than he will gain on the other.

The objection sounds plausible ; it looks almost like being valid, but let us bring it to the test of experience.

Make a list of the names of all the people you know, know with any sort of intimacy, of course, I mean. Then make a desperate effort to be quite honest with yourself, and put a cross against the names of those whom you like best.

I assure you that it will need a desperate effort to do that, for you will find yourself again and again tempted, almost irresistibly, to put that cross opposite the names, not of those whom you really like best, but of those whom you feel you ought to like best, because of their amiable qualities, their unselfishness, or of the gratitude which you feel you owe them for kindnesses and services rendered by them to you in the past.

After you have successfully made that effort you will discover that the persons you have spotted, the persons whom you always meet most gladly, those whose conversation and company are the most in-spiring and revivifying, whose very presence raises your spirits when they are low and keeps them up when they are high—are not the men and women who are shining examples of unselfishness, not the sort who may always be counted upon to subordinate their desires and preferences to the preferences and desires of others, even to yours.

And I doubt very much, though this sounds a cynical thing to say, whether they will be those who have made the most sacrifices, great or small, for your sake, or have rendered you services for which a large measure of your gratitude is due.

No ; as I have said, if you have been really honest, the persons upon whom you have bestowed your Cross of the Legion of Honour will be quite likely, to your own surprise, the robust persons, the persons whose very presence exhales not so much sympathy as virility, the persons of strong will, of very decided preferences, and of a very decided habit of following them, the persons who, in all life's mazes and perplexities, take a line of their own, as we say, and stick to it, not over-solicitous as to what other lines it crosses.

These are the persons you will find you would best like to have beside you in times of sickness or of health, of gladness or of sorrow, of peace or of war. These are the popular persons.

Their popularity is not so paradoxical as at first glance it may appear. These strong souls, who are strong because they follow their preferences, and who follow their preferences because they are strong, are happy people, and happiness is contagious. By just being happy themselves they make you a little happier than you would otherwise be ; and you have the satisfaction of knowing that your gain is by no jot or tittle their loss. When they do anything for you, little or great, you know that in doing it they are not obeying the command of duty or seeking to lay up treasure in heaven, but just pleasing themselves ; and so you can accept that service as freely, as frankly, as it is offered, quit of any little furtive, niggling, annoying sense of obligation.

With the other sort of people, the people with earned reputations for self-sacrifice, who, so far from boldly following their own preferences, for the most part suspect and distrust and turn their backs upon them just because they are their preferences, you, if you are of the better sort, never feel altogether at ease. You feel the extreme likelihood that in serving you they are serving what they conceive to be a Higher Purpose—that they are doing a disagreeable thing more or less because it is disagreeable. One must really be a bit of a curmudgeon, you know, to feel anything but discomfort at being made the occasion of disagreeableness to other people.

I once heard a lecturer on ethics tell an audience of schoolboys that they must never omit to take a cold bath in the morning, no matter how bitter the weather or how strong their disinclination ; not because taking a cold bath was a cleanly thing to do, but because it was an unpleasant thing to do, and one could not do better, he said, than begin the day by doing something unpleasant to oneself.

I daresay he was right. But I confess that when anyone does something unselfish on my behalf it irks me to feel that he is perhaps regarding me as that lecturer would have the schoolboy regard the bath.

That liking which we all of us feel instinctively, spontaneously, for those of our fellows who have the habit of following their own preferences, and of not being over-regardful of ours we, in an odd way, carry into our relations with the animal world. I am not quite sure that we all like cats more than we like dogs ; but I am quite sure that we all respect cats more than we respect dogs.

It is true we do not speak of the cat as the " friend of man," or gush about its fidelity. But, insensibly, and scarce knowing why, we treat the cat as a sort of equal and the dog as a sort of slave. We give way to the cat ; we love to hear it purr. And the reason of the difference we make between the two is, I verily and seriously believe, that we subconsciously recognize in Grimalkin a quality which we would all like to possess in a higher degree than we do, and in Fido a quality which we know we do possess, and deep down in our hearts despise ourselves for possessing.

This difference—shall we say, this moral difference?—between the creature who single-heartedly follows its own preferences and the one who fawningly watches us to see if haply it may discover ours, the ancient wisdom of Old Egypt recognized and acted upon. It made of the cat a god and of the dog a pariah.

From "Essays by Hubert"

ON DOING NOTHING

J. B. PRIESTLEY

I HAD been staying with a friend of mine, an artist and delightfully lazy fellow, at his cottage among the Yorkshire fells, some ten miles from a railway-station ; and as we had been fortunate enough to encounter a sudden spell of really warm weather, day after day we had set off in the morning, taken the nearest moorland track, climbed leisurely until we had reached somewhere about two thousand feet above sea-level, and had then spent long golden afternoons lying flat on our backs—doing nothing. There is no better lounging place than a moor. It is a kind of clean bare antechamber to heaven. Beneath its apparent monotony that offers no immediate excitements, no absorbing drama of sound and colour, there is a subtle variety in its slowly changing patterns of cloud and shadow and tinted horizons, sufficient to keep up a flicker of interest in the mind all day. With its velvety patches, no bigger than a drawing-room carpet, of fine moorland grass, its surfaces invite repose. Its remoteness, its permanence, its old and sprawling indifference to man and his concerns, rest and cleanse the mind. All the noises of the world are drowned in the one monotonous cry of the curlew.

Day after day, then, found us full-stretched upon the moor, looking up at the sky or gazing dreamily at the distant horizon. It is not strictly true, of course, to say that we did absolutely nothing, for we smoked great quantities of tobacco, ate sandwiches and little sticks of chocolate, drank from the cold bubbling streams that spring up from nowhere, gurgle for a few score yards, then disappear again. Occasionally we exchanged a remark or two. But we probably came as close to doing nothing as it is possible for two members of our race. We made nothing, not even any plans ; not a single idea entered our heads ; we did not even indulge in that genial boasting which is the usual pastime of two friendly males in conference. Somewhere, far away, our friends and relatives were humming and bustling, shaping and contriving, planning, disputing, getting, spending ; but we were as gods, solidly occupied in doing nothing, our minds immaculate vacancies. But when our little hour of idling was done and we descended for the last time, as flushed as sunsets, we came down into this world of men and newspaper owners only to discover that we had just been denounced by Mr Gordon Selfridge.

When and where he had been denouncing us I do not know. Nor do I know what hilarious company had invited and received his confidences. Strange things happen at this season, when the unfamiliar sun ripens our eccentricities. It was only last year or the year before that some enterprising person who had organized a conducted tour to the Continent arranged, as a bait for the more intellectual holiday-makers, that a series of lectures should be given to the party by eminent authors at various places *en route*. The happy tourists set out, and their conductor was as good as his word, for behold—at the very first stopping-place Dean Inge gave them an address on the modern love of pleasure. But whether Mr Selfridge had been addressing a crowd of holiday-makers or a solemn

conference of emporium owners, I do not know, but I
do know that he said that he hated laziness more than
anything else and held it the greatest of sins. I believe too that he delivered some judgment on persons
who waste time, but I have forgotten his reasons and
instances and, to be frank, would count it a dis-
graceful waste of time to discover again what they
were. Mr Selfridge did not mention us by name,
but it is hardly possible to doubt that he had us in
mind throughout his attack on idleness. Perhaps he
had had a frantic vision of the pair of us lying flat on
our backs on the moor, wasting time royally while the
world's work waited to be done, and, incidentally, to
be afterwards bought and sold in Mr Selfridge's store.
I hope he had, for the sight should have done him
good ; we are a pleasing spectacle at any time, but
when we are doing nothing it would do any man's
heart good to see us, even in the most fragmentary
and baffling vision. Unfortunately, Mr Selfridge had
probably already made up his mind about the sin, as
he would call it, of laziness, and so was not open to
conviction, was not ready to be pleased. It is a pity,
and all the more so because his views seem to me to
be wrong and quite definitely harmful.

All the evil in this world is brought about by persons who are always up and doing, but do not know
when they ought to be up nor what they ought to be
doing. The devil, I take it, is still the busiest creature
in the universe, and I can quite imagine him denouncing laziness and becoming angry at the smallest
waste of time. In his kingdom, I will wager, nobody
is allowed to do nothing, not even for a single afternoon. The world, we all freely admit, is in a muddle,
but I for one do not think that it is laziness that has
brought it to such a pass. It is not the active virtues

that it lacks but the passive ones ; it is capable of anything but kindness and a little steady thought. There is still plenty of energy in the world (there never were more fussy people about), but most of it is simply misdirected. If, for example, in July 1914, when there was some capital idling weather, everybody, emperors, kings, archdukes, statesmen, generals, journalists, had been suddenly smitten with an intense desire to do nothing, just to hang about in the sunshine and consume tobacco, then we should all have been much better off than we are now. But no, the doctrine of the strenuous life still went unchallenged ; there must be no time wasted ; something must be done. And, as we know, something was done. Again, suppose our statesmen, instead of rushing off to Versailles with a bundle of ill-digested notions and a great deal of energy to dissipate, had all taken a fortnight off, away from all correspondence and interviews and what not, and had simply lounged about on some hillside or other, apparently doing nothing for the first time in their energetic lives, then they might have gone to their so-called Peace Conference and come away again with their reputations still unsoiled and the affairs of the world in good trim. Even at the present time, if half the politicians in Europe would relinquish the notion that laziness is a crime and go away and do nothing for a little space, we should certainly gain by it. Other examples come crowding into the mind. Thus, every now and then, certain religious sects hold conferences ; but though there are evils abroad that are mountains high, though the fate of civilization is still doubtful, the members who attend these conferences spend their time condemning the length of ladies' skirts and the noisiness of dance bands. They would all be better employed lying flat on their backs somewhere, staring at the sky and recovering their mental health.

The idea that laziness is the primary sin and the accompanying doctrine of the strenuous life are very prevalent in America, and we cannot escape the fact that America is an amazingly prosperous country. But neither can we escape the fact that society there is in such a condition that all its best contemporary writers are satirists. Curiously enough, most of the great American writers have not hesitated to praise idleness, and it has often been their faculty for doing nothing and praising themselves for doing it, that has been their salvation. Thus, Thoreau, without his capacity for idling and doing nothing more than appreciate the Milky Way, would be a cold prig ; and Whitman, robbed of his habit of lounging round with his hands in his pockets and his innocent delight in this pastime, would be merely a large-sized ass. Any fool can be fussy and rid himself of energy all over the place, but a man has to have something in him before he can settle down to do nothing. He must have reserves to draw upon, must be able to plunge into strange slow rivers of dream and reverie, must be at heart a poet. Wordsworth, to whom we go when most other poets fail us, knew the value of doing nothing ; nobody, you may say, could do it better ; and you may discover in his work the best account of the matter. He lived long enough to retract most of his youthful opinions, but I do not think that he ever went back on his youthful notion that a man could have no healthier and more spiritualizing employment than idling about and staring at Nature. (It is true that he is very angry in one poem with some gipsies because they had apparently done absolutely nothing from the time he passed them at

I

the beginning of his walk to the time when he passed them again, twelve hours later. But this is racial prejudice, tinged, I suspect, with envy, for though he had not done much, they had done even less.)   If he were alive to-day I have no doubt he would preach his doctrine more fervently and more frequently than ever, and he would probably attack Mr Selfridge and defend us (beginning " Last week they loitered on a lone wide moor ") in a series of capital sonnets, which would not, by the way, attract the slightest attention.   He would tell us that the whole world would be better off if it spent every possible moment it could, these next ten years, lying flat on its back on a moor, doing nothing.   And he would be right.

LETTER-WRITING

W. R. INGE

THE last volume of the new edition of Byron's *Letters*, and the little collection of letters, with an introduction on the history and art of letter-writing, by Professor Saintsbury, will recall the attention of many readers to a delightful branch of literature, which, to all appearance, has had its day. We have often been told that the penny post killed real letter-writing. But the twopenny post does not seem to have improved the quality or to have seriously diminished the quantity of letters which are certainly not literature.

The typewriter and the telephone are enemies of correspondence which we shall always have with us. I have, indeed, a few occasional correspondents, including three theologians, who are, in this respect at least, imitators of Dean Stanley, whose manuscripts were too much even for Mr Murray's compositors. It is a mercy that these divines have taken to the typewriter, but in most cases a typed letter is a chilly and repellent substitute for the written word.

Byron, I believe, said that his handwriting was as bad as his character, which is hardly possible, since his letters have been deciphered ; but, as a rule, I think the writers of good letters have written them legibly.

Worse than the telephone and the postcard is the pose of being overworked. We do not really get through more sound work than our grandfathers ; but we make a conscience of being always in a hurry —unless, indeed, we are trade unionists, with whom the charge of hurrying is a deadly reproach. We can travel much faster than our grandfathers, and accordingly, we waste much more time in going from place to place. Time-saving inventions have much to answer for in shortening our leisure.

These changes, to be sure, ought to encourage the short letter, of which several admirable examples are preserved. The dispatch of a Captain Walton : " Spanish fleet taken and destroyed, as per margin," would have been excellent, if it had been true ; the Spaniards, I believe, said that it was not. A Royal duke is said to have written to an Irish bishop : " Dear Cork,—Please ordain Stanhope.—Yours, York " ; to which the reply was : " Dear York,— Stanhope's ordained.—Yours, Cork."

It is said that Archbishop Temple once received a letter from an officious correspondent, enclosing two utterances of the Archbishop which flatly contradicted each other, and asking for an explanation. The reply was : " Dear Sir,—Both were right."

I have heard (but I don't believe this story) that during the War the Foreign Office was obliged to employ one or two temporary clerks whose training had been commercial rather than diplomatic. A dignified foreign ambassador was astonished to receive the following missive : " Dear Sir,—Yours to hand, and contents noted. Our Lord C—— has the matter in hand."

As a last example of the short letter—a masterpiece —a father told his son at school that he was too busy to read long letters, and requested the boy to be brief. The answer was a model of terseness : " S.O.S.,

L.S.D., R.S.V.P." The first two of these are old stories, long before the days of postcards.

The long letter is not extinct, but in my experience it is confined to that amazing species of cranks, who, without any introduction or excuse, cover whole quires of paper with epistolary essays addressed to men who happen for the time to be in the public eye, expounding at length their views on theology, politics, and what not, and apparently expect their victims to read and answer them. Really interesting letters, which make breakfast a pleasure, are rare indeed.

Professor Saintsbury does justice to the ancient Romans as the founders of good letter-writing. It is a pity that he has not given us one or two specimens of Cicero. Cicero's are admirable letters, brimful of matter, whereas Mme de Sévigné is as good at writing cleverly about nothing as a French cook is at making dishes out of nothing. Pliny is another admirable correspondent, and a most estimable gentleman, as he wishes us to observe.

But the eighteenth century was the golden age of letter-writing, both in England and in France. The French are right, perhaps, in thinking that Mme de Sévigné has never been surpassed ; but if we consider matter as well as manner, some of our English writers are more interesting. Pope is amazingly clever, but spiteful and disingenuous beyond description. And what are we to think of a man who could append to a sort of love-letter the request, " When this letter is printed for the wit of it, pray take care that what is underlined be printed in a different character"?

Swift, that savage and unholy genius, as Lord Morley calls him, wrote masses of letters to two un-lucky ladies whom he loved in a morbid and unmanly fashion. Brilliant as the *Letters to Stella* are, I cannot

agree with Professor Saintsbury that Swift was " one
of the greatest lovers in the world." He had no full-
blooded love to give.

Cowper, the poet, is one of the very best letter-
writers. When not under the cloud of religious
melancholy he was the most genial and affectionate
of men, and his judgments on public affairs are re-
markably shrewd for a man of his habits.

Horace Walpole is not a favourite of mine. He was
a selfish and self-indulgent fellow, battening on rich
sinecures, who evidently wrote to show how clever he
was. There is not much to show that he really cared
about his correspondents.

Far more delightful, to my mind, are the letters of
Gray, poet, scholar, and recluse, who gave his correspondents the best of a well-stored mind, and is
particularly good in describing his travels—not an
easy thing to do really well. His letters are like very
good talk, which is what letters ought to be.

For this reason some of the best letter-writers have
been women. Lady Mary Wortley Montagu, in the
eighteenth century, is admirable ; and in the nineteenth two women who married geniuses, Mrs Carlyle
and Mrs Browning, wrote even better letters than
their husbands. Mrs Carlyle was a little spiteful, but
this is not an unmixed drawback in a letter.

Shelley, Keats, and Byron are all famous letter-
writers. I prefer Shelley of the three. Byron is revealed in this last volume as a very imperfect kind of
gentleman. He not only kissed and told, but seems
to prefer the latter to the former.

Fitzgerald, the translator of Omar Khayyám, is a
prince among letter-writers. It is really a good thing
that a few able men should be content to be very
leisurely. Their work gains in quality, and they have

time, if they choose, to write letters which deserve to be classics.

The modern biography is usually swollen to twice its proper size by unnecessary and dull letters. To print love-letters is an outrage ; and nobody wants to know the first impressions of Lucerne, dutifully written home by a young traveller. A biographer once confided to me that all the really interesting letters had had to be left out.

It only remains to mention that peculiar branch of letter-writing—letters sent to newspapers. It once fell to my lot to propose the prosperity of a newspaper which had been giving me a bad time in its correspondence columns. I congratulated the editor on his wisdom in allowing the least intelligent of his readers to let off steam in this way. Considering the letters which are printed—say, in the religious weeklies—one wonders what the rejected addresses can be like.

We must hope, without much confidence, that the graceful and gentle art of letter-writing may have another flowering time among us.

From "Lay Thoughts of a Dean"

ON BEING HARD UP

JEROME K. JEROME

IT is a most remarkable thing. I sat down with the full intention of writing something clever and original ; but for the life of me I can't think of something clever and original—at least, not at this moment. The only thing I can think about now is being hard up. I suppose having my hands in my pockets has made me think about this. I always do sit with my hands in my pockets, except when I am in the company of my sisters, my cousins, or my aunts ; and they kick up such a shindy—I should say expostulate so eloquently upon the subject —that I have to give in and take them out—my hands I mean. The chorus to their objections is that it is not gentlemanly. I am hanged if I can see why. I could understand its not being considered gentlemanly to put your hands in other people's pockets (especially by the other people), but how, O ye sticklers for what looks this and what looks that, can putting his hands in his own pockets make a man less gentle ? Perhaps you are right, though. Now I come to think of it, I have heard some people grumble most savagely when doing it. But they were mostly old gentlemen. We young fellows, as a rule, are never quite at ease unless we have our hands in our pockets. We are awkward and shifty. We are like what a music-hall Lion Comique would be without his opera hat, if such a thing can be imagined. But let us put our hands in our trousers' pockets, and let there be some small change in the right-hand one and a bunch of keys in the left, and we will face a female post-office clerk.

It is a little difficult to know what to do with your hands, even in your pockets, when there is nothing else there. Years ago, when my whole capital would occasionally come down to " what in town the people call a bob," I would recklessly spend a penny of it, merely for the sake of having the change, all in coppers, to jingle. You don't feel nearly so hard up with elevenpence in your pocket as you do with a shilling. Had I been " la-di-da," that impecunious youth about whom we superior folk are so sarcastic, I would have changed my penny for two ha'pennies.

I can speak with authority on the subject of being hard up. I have been a provincial actor. If further evidence be required, which I do not think likely, I can add that I have been a gentleman " connected with the press." I have lived on fifteen shillings a week. I have lived a week on ten, owing the other five ; and I have lived for a fortnight on a greatcoat.

It is wonderful what an insight into domestic economy being really hard up gives one. If you want to find out the value of money, live on fifteen shillings a week, and see how much you can put by for clothes and recreation. You will find out that it is worth while to wait for the farthing change, that it is worth while to walk a mile to save a penny, that a glass of beer is a luxury to be indulged in only at rare intervals, and that a collar can be worn for four days.

Try it just before you get married. It will be excellent practice. Let your son and heir try it before sending him to college. He won't grumble at a hundred a year pocket money then. There are some people to whom it would do a world of good. There is that delicate blossom, who can't drink any claret under ninety-four, and who would as soon think of dining off cats' meat as off plain roast mutton. You do come across these poor wretches now and then, though, to the credit of humanity, they are principally confined to that fearful and wonderful society known only to lady novelists. I never hear of one of these creatures discussing a menu card but I feel a mad desire to drag him off to the bar of some common East End public-house, and cram a sixpenny dinner down his throat—beefsteak pudding, fourpence ; potatoes, a penny ; half a pint of porter, a penny. The recollection of it (and the mingled fragrance of beer, tobacco, and roast pork generally leaves a vivid impression) might induce him to turn up his nose a little less frequently in the future at everything that is put before him. Then, there is that generous party, the cadger's delight, who is so free with his small change, but who never thinks of paying his debts. It might teach even him a little common sense. " I always give the waiter a shilling. One can't give the fellow less, you know," explained a young Government clerk with whom I was lunching the other day in Regent Street. I agreed with him as to the utter impossibility of making it elevenpence ha'penny ; but, at the same time, I resolved to one day decoy him to an eating-house I remembered near Covent Garden, where the waiter, for the better discharge of his duties, goes about in his shirt-sleeves—and very dirty sleeves they are too, when it gets near the end of the month. I know that waiter. If my friend gives him anything beyond a penny, the man will insist on shaking hands with him then and there, as a mark of his esteem : of that I feel sure.

There have been a good many funny things said and written about hardupishness, but the reality is not funny, for all that. It is not funny to have to haggle over pennies. It isn't funny to be thought mean and stingy. It isn't funny to be shabby, and to be ashamed of your address. No, there is nothing at all funny in poverty—to the poor. It is hell upon earth to a sensitive man ; and many a brave gentleman, who would have faced the labours of Hercules, has had his heart broken by its petty miseries.

It is not the actual discomforts themselves that are hard to bear. Who would mind roughing it a bit if that were all it meant ? What cared Robinson Crusoe for a patch on his trousers ?—Did he wear trousers ? I forget ; or did he go about like he does in the pantomimes ? What did it matter to him if his toes did stick out of his boots ? and what if his umbrella was a cotton one, so long as it kept the rain off ? His shabbiness did not trouble him : there were none of his friends round about to sneer at him.

Being poor is a mere trifle. It is being known to be poor that is the sting. It is not cold that makes a man without a greatcoat hurry along so quickly. It is not all shame at telling lies—which he knows will not be believed—that makes him turn so red when he informs you that he considers greatcoats unhealthy, and never carries an umbrella on principle. It is easy enough to say that poverty is no crime. No ; if it were men wouldn't be ashamed of it. It is a blunder, though, and is punished as such. A poor man is despised the whole world over ; despised as much by a Christian as by a lord, as much by a demagogue as by a footman, and not all the copybook maxims ever set for ink-stained youth will make him respected. Appearances *are* everything, so far as human opinion goes : and the man who will walk down Piccadilly arm in arm with the most notorious scamp in London, provided he is a well-dressed one, will slink up a back street to say a couple of words to a seedy-looking gentleman. And the seedy-looking gentleman knows this—no one better—and will go a mile round to avoid meeting an acquaintance. Those that knew him in his prosperity need never trouble themselves to look the other way. He is a thousand times more anxious that they should not see him than they can be ; and as to their assistance, there is nothing he dreads more than the offer of it. All he wants is to be forgotten ; and in this respect he is generally fortunate enough to get what he wants.

One becomes used to being hard up, like one becomes used to everything else, by the help of that wonderful old homœopathic doctor, Time. You can tell at a glance the difference between the old hand and the novice ; between the case-hardened man who has been used to shift and struggle for years, and the poor devil of a beginner, striving to hide his misery, and in a constant agony of fear lest he should be found out. Nothing shows this difference more clearly than the way in which each will pawn his watch. As the poet says somewhere : " True ease in pawning comes from art, not chance." The one goes into his ' Uncle's ' with as much composure as he would into his tailor's—very likely with more. The assistant is even civil and attends to him at once, to the great indignation of the lady in the next box, who, however, sarcastically observes that she don't mind being kept waiting " if it is a reg'lar customer." Why, from the pleasant and businesslike manner in which the transaction is carried out, it might be a large purchase in the Three per Cents. Yet what a piece of work a man makes of his first ' pop.' A boy popping his first question is confidence itself compared with him. He hangs about outside the shop, until he has succeeded in attracting the attention of all the loafers in the neighbourhood, and has aroused strong suspicions in the mind of the policeman on the beat. At last after a careful examination of the windows, made for the purpose of impressing the bystanders with the notion that he is going in to purchase a diamond bracelet or some such trifle, he enters, trying to do so with a careless swagger, and giving himself really the air of a member of the swell mob. When inside, he speaks in so low a voice as to be perfectly inaudible, and has to say it all over again. When, in the course of his rambling conversation about a " friend " of his, the word " lend " is reached, he is promptly told to go up the court on the right, and take the first door round the corner. He comes out of the shop with a face that you could easily light a cigarette at, and firmly under the impression that the whole population of the district is watching him. When he does get to the right place he has forgotten his name and address, and is in a general condition of hopeless imbecility. Asked in a severe tone how he came by " this," he stammers and contradicts himself, and it is only a miracle if he does not confess to having stolen it that very day. He is thereupon informed that they don't want anything to do with his sort, and that he had better get out of this as quickly as possible, which he does, recollecting nothing more until he finds himself three miles off, without the slightest knowledge how he got there.

By the way, how awkward it is, though, having to depend on public-houses and churches for the time. The former are generally too fast, and the latter too

slow.   Besides which, your efforts to get a glimpse of
the public-house clock from the outside, are attended
with great difficulties.   If you gently push the swing
door ajar and peer in, you draw upon yourself the
contemptuous looks of the barmaid, who at once puts
you down in the same category with area sneaks and
cadgers.   You also create a certain amount of agita-
tion among the married portion of the customers.
You don't see the clock, because it is behind the door ;
and, in trying to withdraw quietly, you jamb your
head.   The only other method is to jump up and
down outside the window.   After this latter proceed-
ing, however, if you do not bring out a banjo and
commence to sing, the youthful inhabitants of the
neighbourhood, who have gathered round in expec-
tation, become disappointed.

I should like to know, too, by what mysterious law
of nature it is that, before you have left your watch
" to be repaired " half an hour, some one is sure to
stop you in the street and conspicuously ask you the
time.   Nobody even feels the slightest curiosity on the
subject when you've got it on.

Dear old ladies and gentlemen, who know nothing
about being hard up—and may they never, bless their
grey old heads—look upon the pawnshop as the last
stage of degradation ; but those who know it better
(and my readers have, no doubt, noticed this themselves), are often surprised, like the little boy who
dreamed he went to heaven, at meeting so many
people there that they never expected to see.   For
my part, I think it a much more independent course
than borrowing from friends, and I always try to
impress this upon those of my acquaintance who
incline towards " wanting a couple of pounds till the
day after to-morrow."   But they won't all see it.

One of them once remarked that he objected to the principle of the thing. I fancy if he had said it was the interest that he objected to he would have come nearer to the truth ; twenty-five per cent. certainly does come heavy.

There are degrees in being hard up. We are all hard up, more or less—most of us more. Some are hard up for a thousand pounds ; some for a shilling. Just at this moment I am hard up myself for a fiver. I only want it for a day or two. I should be certain of paying it back within a week at the outside, and if any lady or gentleman among my readers would kindly lend it me, I should be very much obliged indeed. They could send it to me, under cover to Messrs Field and Tuer, only, in such case, please let the envelope be carefully sealed. I would give you my I.O.U. as security.

From "The Idle Thoughts of an Idle Fellow"

THE TOY THEATRE

GERALD BULLETT

OLIVER WENDELL HOLMES'S Autocrat was a little wide of the mark when he implied that every man represents a trinity of persons and no more. His analysis of a hypothetical John was accurate as far as it went, but it did not go far enough. He tells us that a dialogue between John and Thomas engages six personalities : (1) The real John ; known only to his Maker. (2) John's ideal John ; never the real one, and often very unlike him. (3) Thomas's ideal John ; never the real John, nor John's John, but often very unlike either. Thomas contributes a similar trio. All three are treated as constants though there is surely every reason to suppose that they are variable. They are all in a perpetual state of flux, and No. 2, which looks so simple, constitutes a host that cannot be numbered. For everybody who is at all introspective, and more particularly everybody who has the trick of self-detachment, knows himself to possess as many personalities as acquaintances. For each of my friends I possess a special set of reactions, a special voice, manner, attitude of mind. At the mere approach of another the appropriate personality pops up in me like a Jack-in-the-box. The difference is not superficial : it is more apparent to me than to anybody else. It is, therefore, a *real* difference, appearance being the only reality

worth bothering about. I do not merely seem different : I feel so, and am so.

  If you reflect on this matter for a moment, you get
some surprising results. Consider your own case.
Robinson, you will remember, has always regarded
you as rather a dark horse, a clever fellow, a master
of impressive though incomprehensible *double entente.*
Consequently, whenever Robinson comes to see you,
you are conscious of a mysterious inward change.
And this change within is reflected in a change without.   You do not actively conspire to deceive
Robinson : the mask slips over your face by none of
your contriving.   You find yourself looking upon the
world through cynical eyes.   It is a new, queer world,
and you want to make sly fun of it.   This end you
achieve by a system of raised eyebrows, inscrutable
smiles, subtleties of intonation, and a certain brevity
of speech.   It is not what you say that is so witty, so
cruel.   Indeed, you say so little that another man—
Jones, for example—would suppose you to be out of
sorts. A good fellow, Jones, in his way ; but he
lacks that sensitiveness to atmosphere which makes
Robinson such a charming companion.   Robinson,
as well you know, can detect a delicate tinge of irony
even in the monosyllable with which you acknowledge
his remark about the weather.   By a simple " yes "
or " no," uttered in just the right tone, you have put
the weather in its place.   Robinson chuckles in delightful appreciation of your criticism.   Presently he
begins to tell you how at the Club last night . . .
You interrupt him.   " Ah," you say, " the Club ! "
Three words bleak enough in themselves, yet their
effect is devastating.   The Club is at once annihilated,
blown sky-high by the gunpowder of your personality,
scattered to limbo by the wind of your wit.   The

K

place it occupied is desolate. Wild beasts of the
desert shall lie there ; and owls shall dwell there,
and satyrs shall dance there. And all because your
lips curled a little in uttering the words, " Ah, the
Club ! " It is something of a responsibility, this new
personality of yours. You have become such a terrible fellow that it behoves you to wield your power
with restraint. That realization adds the zest of peril
to every moment you spend with dear old Robinson.
But you do not shrink from the responsibility : you
enjoy it. And when Robinson has gone, leaving you
with only the ghost of the self you had foisted on him,
you still remember him with gratitude. " I like
Robinson," you say to yourself. But what you like
is not Robinson at all : it is that engaging, that
brilliant creature in yourself which the presence of
Robinson evokes. It is commonly admitted that the
cat who rubs his face against that of his mistress is
caressing, not his mistress, but himself. And this is
true not only of feline caresses. " An hour in Robinson's company does me good," you may add. " I
always enjoy myself."

That last sentence indicates a profound truth which
has possibly escaped you. You do indeed enjoy
yourself : that is to say, you enjoy whichever of your
multitudinous selves happens to hold the floor at
the moment. Yourself is the only thing you ever do
enjoy, because it is the only thing you experience.
For Robinson, for the ultimate and mysterious reality
called Robinson, you have no feeling at all, whether
of affection or hostility. You have never come in
contact with him, hidden away as he is, like every
mortal creature, in an impregnable tower of isolation.
The same is true of Jones and Brown. Your Jones-
personality is perhaps rather dogmatic, and ponti-

fical, with a habit of indulging in heavy platitudes about the safety of the Empire and the great heart o democracy, although Jones himself, so far as you can see, is not at all that kind of man. With Brown you are the genial man-about-town, full of inside information about things of which you are totally ignorant. Indeed you have, it is clear, far more personalities than you can count. With one you play bears with your baby ; with another you reprove the cook ; with a third you attend a meeting of your Board of Directors. The differences are not all so obvious as these ; but some difference, however subtle, there always is. Every time you button up your overcoat in an east wind you preserve from possible extinction a hundred and one little actors. And when you are alone, what then ? Are the actors quiescent ? I doubt it. Certainly they have not ceased to exist, for the least disturbance of your solitude will bring one of them dancing upon the stage.

For I must break it to you, with such tact and tenderness as I can muster, that you who have for so long imagined yourself to be a single human personality are at your best a mob ; and at your worst, in moments of indecision, you are a mere riot. You are a Toy Theatre, a travelling show, a variety entertainment. As to who is the Stage Manager, that is a question that would lead me too deeply into metaphysics, and possibly into theology, where you would very properly refuse to follow me. If you consider yourself affronted by what I have felt it my duty to tell you, I apologize, but without withdrawing a word of it. If you feel desolated, I urge you to remember that I am in a similar plight myself. I have said, in effect, that we, every mother's son of us, are always acting a part : but this does not convict us of universal hypocrisy.   Each personality, while it holds the stage, may be perfectly sincere, though it is asking too much that the entire theatrical company shall be in perfect agreement upon everything.   Sincerity, it cannot be denied, is the most difficult and delicate of the arts. Perhaps one comes nearest to achieving it in the act of writing an essay.

OF VARIOUS OCCASIONS

HOME FOR THE HOLIDAYS

J. T. ST LOE STRACHEY

FORTUNATELY, the arrangement of the schoolboys' Summer and Winter exodus is a much easier task than formerly, and there is comparatively little difficulty in managing that those who are bound for a common destination shall travel together. The viatorial vagaries of which a boy travelling alone and given to wool-gathering, or to becoming lost in the blood-curdling exploits of pirate chiefs and their rakish schooners, is capable, are almost incredible. The power of not arriving at his destination which he develops on such occasions is positively portentous. If he has to make a cross journey with just enough time to catch his train nicely he almost certainly misses it, while if he has a good hour to spare the result is much the same, for he is then as likely as not to start off on some external expedition, which brings him back to the station long after the hour at which he ought to have been there. Then, too, he discovers endless possibilities of getting into the wrong portions of trains, of fancying that the slip coach is " the one next the engine," and of getting left behind owing to his having become absorbed in the voracious and indiscriminate consumption of mock-turtle soup, buns, hot coffee, chocolate creams, and bottled ale in the refreshment room.

For some reason, however, not easily explained, a

party of boys travelling together do not seem nearly so liable to these accidents. Whether it is that a sense of responsibility becomes abnormally developed in the oldest member of the party, and that he checks the errant instincts of the rest of the band, and recalls their minds to the grim necessities of junctions and the "forward part of the train," or whether a knot of young gentlemen in round jackets and Eton collars attracts the special notice of the guard, and ensures the supervision of the officials, it is impossible to say with certainty. Whatever is the reason, the fact remains that parties show a tendency to get home, if not always to time, at least before nightfall, while individuals travelling alone very often fare like the Irishman who was wont to complain that, however early he started, he never arrived anywhere at all.

Dickens, in one of his letters, asks how it is that boys home for the holidays contrive to spend the whole day clumping downstairs in apparently at least six pairs of the thickest boots. This curious and interesting problem is at every holiday season presented to the British parent, as well as a thousand other strange and inexplicable habits of his male offspring. It is the charm—or, as a misanthrope would say, the curse—of boyhood never to be able to do anything in the way that it is done by the rest of the world. In this very matter of the stairs, for instance, the unvarying singularity of boys is universally to be noticed. No boy can ever manage to accomplish a simple descent or ascent. His movements, whether going up or going down, are conducted with an earnestness and vigour which it would be quite impossible for any grown-up person to imitate. Putting aside the *glissade* on the banisters, or down the waxed and varnished edges of the treads as belonging more properly to the department of home gymnastics, the most ordinary system, at least for coming down, is that which may best be described as the flying leap— four steps at a time, with an occasional cannon against the wall to vary the monotony of the descent.

If, however, there is sickness in the house a boy of good feeling will abandon this method of precipitating himself as a sort of human avalanche from the top landing to the dining-room floor, and will adopt quite another plan. Probably he has been admonished at some time or other to go down quietly one step at a time, and, making use of this suggestion, he proceeds to carry it out to the letter. Seizing the banisters with both hands, he jumps heavily from the first step, alighting firmly upon his heels on the next, to rebound thence to the one below, and so on till he reaches the bottom. This action, which sounds for all the world like the ghastly antics of some bewitched coffin which has reared itself on end, and resolved to appear at family prayers, is probably that to which the author of *Pickwick* alludes.

At any rate, the system is exceedingly widespread, and is, we firmly believe, considered by many young gentlemen between the ages of eight and fourteen as a specially merciful method of transferring their persons from one storey to another. Next to the ability displayed by boys in getting tones undreamt of by ordinary performers out of the front and kitchen stairs is their talent for shaking the whole house by merely walking across an upstairs floor. Paterfamilias, who weighs, perhaps, fourteen stone, when he treads the boards of his dressing-room makes no perceptible vibration. But let Jack, who cannot possibly weigh half that amount, be sent to bring down a book for his father, and anyone in the back drawing-room would imagine that at least a dozen mad elephants had been let loose above. Yet Jack, in all probability, made no special effort to be noisy, and at most crossed the floor to get to the book-case by stepping only on the white squares in the carpet.

No doubt these and plenty of other physical and mental peculiarities of the schoolboy will at first give pleasure rather than the reverse at home. English parents are much too fond of their children not to forget such little annoyances in the pleasure of having their boys home again, and of observing how clever, handsome, or jolly-looking they have grown, and how extraordinarily like they are to their fathers, mothers, grandfathers, or grandmothers, or, indeed, to all their relatives, immediate and remote. For several days the veritable tempests of noise that sweep down the stairs and thunder through the front hall will be pronounced " quite cheerful," and there will be a general agreement among the elder members of the family that the house is never a bit like home till the boys come back.

Little by little, however, the charm will wear off, and though the sight of their children will, in reality, be just as much a happiness to their parents as before, a feeling will begin to grow up that there are objections to the sense of perpetual motion which seems somehow to pervade the house. Though the mother of the family would in all probability refuse to admit it, she at last begins to find the banging of doors, without the slightest intermission, a little trying. Then, too, the father of the family, though, theoreti-cally, he may enjoy nothing better than being a boy again among his boys, discovers that it is rather nervous work never to be sure that when he comes round a corner he will not encounter some missile which, although meant " only for Jack," is equally capable of ' stinging up ' the author of Jack's being.

One of Mr Bret Harte's characters complains quaintly, but not unreasonably, that " this dodging of pillows imparts but small ease to the style," and if Paterfamilias' vocations are of a literary nature the truth of the remark may come home to him with special force during the holidays. To receive a broadside from a bolster battery, meant to hold the maids in check, when one has gone upstairs to look out a quotation in Milton, is almost certain to destroy all suavity of phrase and period. When, again, there is a wet August, and little or no going out is possible, the lot of parents caged up with three or four boys is not exactly a happy one. It is only natural that what ordinary fathers and mothers detest more than anything else in the world is having to decide which of their offspring is in the wrong in a domestic quarrel. But wet days are certain to bring about such home broils, in which it is very difficult for the parent to intervene except by the rough and ready—though often essentially unjust—method of punishing, or at any rate reprimanding, the one who happens to have emerged least hurt from the scuffle.

Though the plan has about it a kind of natural equity—a sort of ' equality of sacrifice,' to borrow a phrase from the regions of finance—which may be supposed to recommend it to the youthful mind, Paterfamilias usually dislikes employing it. In fact, all attempts to administer justice to schoolboys are peculiarly unpleasant, since their code of honour necessarily renders it impossible for either combatant to make known, even in the slightest degree, the rights of the dispute. Add to this that the girls of the family, who were petted by their brothers when they first came home, are, towards the end of the Vacation, in obedience to the universal law that familiarity breeds contempt, mercilessly teased, fagged, and harried. If we take this into account, and remember, too, that the servants who to begin with thought nothing more amusing than the young gentlemen's apple-pie beds and booby traps, have reached the verge of mutiny by the fifth week, and it is not difficult to realize that the beginning of the next half is greeted with as much joy as was the end of the last.

With boys who go to Day-schools it is quite possible to arrange a *modus vivendi* without making them unduly good and quiet. But the holidays of the boy at the Boarding-school have too much of the nature of a Saturnalia to make them pleasant for parents, at any rate after the first month. When the fourth week is past the coming term is looked forward to with undisguised delight.

From "From Grave to Gay"

ON GOING BACK

GERALD GOULD

OME day I'll go back to Oxford——"
That is a line of poetry—of the new poetry,
I suppose, since it doesn't seem to scan on
any known principle, and cannot be expected to
rhyme with anything, and appears to express a very
simple, a very commonplace intention. I can see the
critic (if he is not himself an Oxford man) wrinkling
a deprecatory nose at it, and declaring that it ought
not to be called poetry at all. I can only say it is
poetry to me.

" Some day I'll go back to Oxford——"
If one only could !

Of course, I am using the word Oxford in a generic
sense. *Your* Oxford may be Cambridge, or Paris, or
London, or Rome, or Southend, or Thrums. Any
place where you have been happy, where you have
been young, where others have been young with you
(this last is the most important consideration of all)
—any place from which the world has looked friendly
and full of promise—any place to which you can
never get back—is the Oxford of the soul.

People often tease themselves with the question
whether they would like to have their lives over again.
It is a meaningless question, because the human
imagination cannot conceive a precise repetition of
anything : if you try to picture that other self of
yours, the self you were twenty years ago, you find

at once that what you are really picturing is your
present self dressed up in the past shape. But man
is not a rational animal ; and he persists in desiring
what he cannot get and cannot even imagine.

The author of the line with which we began is
Mr Humbert Wolfe. And he puts his imagination
to work ; he sees himself as he used, or thinks he
used, to be :

> The porter will smile at my waistcoat and my ways,
> when I'm not looking, as he used to in other days.

He sees the journey. Acton, Ealing, Reading, Did-
cot at last, Radley. . . . He pretends that his blood
" doesn't jump like a fish." When he gets out, there
are none of these new-fangled taxis to remind him :

> I shall step out silently, and take a cab,
> that slides along the cobbles like a wounded crab.
> I'll say to the cabman, " Wadham," and then sit
> perfectly still, but my body will be lit
> like a great house with candles.

And he ends as he began—" Some day I'll go back
to Oxford——"

The beauty and pathos of the poem, of course,
depend on the fact that he won't. Not like that, at
any rate. When one really goes back to Oxford, in
the flesh, one is a ghost on the old stairs, and the
streets are full of strange, alien, cheerful creatures in
the most impossible kind of trousers. I remember
the lines of Mr Belloc, another Oxford poet :

> I will not try the reach again,
>   I will not set my sail alone,
> To moor a boat bereft of men
>   At Yarnton's tiny docks of stone.

One cannot go back ; but one can do no harm by
remembering. Another poem of Mr Wolfe's, the one

called *Denmark*, takes my memory back much further than to Oxford :

> O little fir-tree of Denmark, I passed you by, but I guessed
> what star of an unborn Christmas waited against your breast—
> somewhere the glass-balls are waiting, and the unlit candles
> glisten
> somewhere, and somewhere the children unborn are singing !
> oh listen !

I suppose your childhood, like Mr Wolfe's, like mine, is bound up with that fir-tree of Hans Andersen's. We all of us read the story long before we can possibly know what it means. The tree grew, you remember, " where the warm sun and the fresh air made a sweet resting-place " ; but it was not happy, " it wished so much to be like its tall companions." " Oh," it cried, " if I could but keep on growing tall and old ! There is nothing else worth caring for in the world ! "

Its companions were cut down and taken away to the sea ; and the fir-tree wanted to go too.

> " Rejoice in thy youth," said the sunbeam ; " rejoice in thy fresh growth, and the young life that is in thee."
> And the wind kissed the tree, and the dew watered it with tears ; but the fir-tree regarded them not.

More companions were cut down and taken away ; and these went to the houses of the town, and, as the sparrows reported, " were dressed up in the most splendid manner." And finally came the turn of the discontented fir-tree itself ; and, after much pain and sorrow (which somehow had not been part of the anticipation) it found itself adorned with little bags cut out of coloured paper, and gilded apples and walnuts, and hundreds of red, blue, and white tapers.

You remember the downfall—how the fir-tree was reduced, in the lumber-room, to telling the mice about its youth ; and how it reflected : " After all, those were happy days " ; and how in the end it was chopped up. " Now all was past ; the tree's life was past, and the story also—for all stories must come to an end at last."

When I reread that story now, it seems to me the most beautiful story in the world ; in a sense, indeed, the only story in the world. And its moral is that, though one can never go back, it is worth while to have been.

From "The Return to the Cabbage"

A SENTIMENTAL JOURNEY

IVOR BROWN

QUARTER of a century is a phrase with an epochal ring, and these last five and twenty years have altered the world more than most. Empires have waxed and waned ; motor-cars have altered the whole face of travel and the whole scale of British distances ; a penny has become a half-penny, and the char-à-banc has crashed its way through the silent austerities of the Scottish Sabbath. But much of Scotland stands exactly where it did. Here in the North-east, whither I have made my sentimental journey, the land and sea yield the old harvests of grain and herring. The plough that has not altered since Homer told its shape and motion is not to suffer change while a boy grows up. The sea shows more of steam and less of sail, but evolution has obliged Tennessee by signally failing to leave new marks on herring and haddock, rabbit and hare. Had I been a London boy, I could hardly go in search of my youth. For the horses of the green Atlas bus that took me to Lord's have vanished, and no more is the effortless beauty of J. T. Hearne's bowling to be observed. But here I can go to " the games " last visited in 1900 and they will be held in the same " haugh " ; the same dancing-master will sit on the judgment bench to nod gravely at the same flings and sword-dances. The pipes will be mournful and brisk with the same airs, and tea-time will bring the same

neat bag of cakes.   True, the programme hinted at the
presence of the Abertochty " jazz band."   But what's
in a name ?   As of old there were fiddlers three.

The conditions, as they say, are eminently suitable.
Here one may indeed go in search of one's youth and
reconstruct in the tranquillity of a sunny afternoon
the emotions of a very small boy.   Of course it is
all much smaller than one's memory.   A mile has
dwindled to a furlong, a forest to a copse, a torrent
to a trickle.   The trout that were Tritons are now to
be seen as flickering minnows in the shallows under
the bridge.   A mountain has shrunk to a hillock.   It
doesn't do, this retracing of boyhood's steps.   One
knew, of course, that looking backward is like looking
through an opera-glass reversed.   But the distortion
is worse than one imagined.   One shouldn't have
gone.   The return has been a cowardly assault upon
romance, a butchering of innocent memories.   Far
better have left the old house to be, in mind's eye,
grandiose, mysterious, abounding in dark possibilities ;
in short, the half-menacing, half-entrancing monster
that it used to be.   Far better have left to the gardens
their flattering spaciousness of boyhood's vision, to
the wood its pristine mystery of cavernous and black
allure.

But one has done the deed.   There it all lies, plain-
set in smiling sunlight, a diminished Paradise.   It is
just a piece of Eastern Scotland, that frank and self-
explanatory countryside which rolls an open bosom
to the plain, straightforward sea.   No Celtic twilights,
tortuous lochs, and peaks that stab the mist are here
to make adult reason concede a tremor to romance.
Good farming trims the landscape ; grey, orderly
walls keep watch over pasture, roots, and oats.   Here
and there the rising ground soars out of man's control

and green fields admit their limitations and march peaceably with heather. Here the hillside turns to fir plantation, there to empty purple acres. But the wildness, the strangeness, the beckoning immensities of those old days have shrivelled and departed. Boyhood was too small for Ordnance maps and the withering accuracies of the measuring-rod. It made its own mileage, forged its own contours, made and named and ruled its mountain range. Compute it now coldly at "one inch to mile" and a kingdom turns to a crofter's holding. Yet within this nutshell moved a king of infinite space. Perhaps not king ; a princeling were more accurate.

The owls have gone from the quivering pinewood ; no heron flaps its pondering course along the burn. The coneys we have always with us, and their tribe at least is slow to dwindle. The gamekeeper has gone from the lodge, and he who knew the haunts of beast and bird now peddles bull's-eyes and half-pounds of tea. He is an injured man. Somebody started a war, and there has been no need for small estates since then. A nice range of red deer, grouse, and salmon will fetch a doubled price from merchant princes, for we are not all paupers at holiday-time. But the solid "mixed shooting" with nothing showy about it and a four-square chunk of masonry to maintain attracts no bidders now. The lawns grow weeds, and the gamekeeper digs potatoes until the shop bell rings, and then he must weigh out another quarter of sweeties. He knows it is all wrong, but he says very little. He never goes near the house from which he has been driven. For relaxation he has his parlour, and there he sits with all the immobility of the soil-bound peasant looking at nothing, unless it is the past. "You'll notice the sea has worked in a lot," he says. " It's beating the land by a yard a year. It'll tak' a' the links. There's changes everywhere."

Yet was this visitation altogether a blundering folly ? Has the sentimental journey proved altogether a wanton outrage upon sentiment ? No ; it has its powers of reassurance, its compensations, and its fair suggestions. The woods have lost their wonder, and their darkness is a plain, unghosted thing. But beauty has crept in. Boyhood never saw that. Boyhood never knew the exquisite proportion of this countryside in which the elements of sea, moor, tilth, pasture, and copse have been dispensed as though by some inspired chemist of landscape. The place does yield its reparations and pays them in the currency of the eye's delight. How fitly the house lifts up its native stone, grey, unassuming, comfortably set ! How lightly the bridge jumps the burn and leads to the village and the mellow-gardened manse ! The sense of a desert has departed and the sense of a civilization has come in. If one no longer looks for eagles in the skies or marauders in the glades, one can look for shapeliness in homes and handsomeness in everything. And it is a handsome country garnished by diligence and fruitful under discipline. The grey-beard who comes down from his farm to judge the piping and dancing at the village games will not whine to you about bad times. He has the measure of the soil and of his agrarian competitors ; he has whipped his land into a clean prosperity, and his cattle are known and feared at the Royal Northern Show. His sons have gone to the university, but he is just a little doubtful about the teaching at the village academy. They want a better man, and, from the sound of his voice, they mean to get one. To judge the pibrochs is the limit of his surrender to

Gaelic dreaming. His youngest boy is going to be as great a man of medicine as ever went south from Aberdeen. He goes on Sunday to the kirk, thinks little of the minister, and has no qualms.

It was once a land of giants, black-bearded men, who came up from the coastal fisheries and sometimes took a small boy in their boat to see the odd harvest of their nets. It was full of dark pools and distant heights, of birds and animals, of hopes and panics and surprises. It is not at all like that now. Boy Scouts encamp themselves where once was desolation. The burn trills equally through small and genial copses. The fields run up to the heather, and the heather, a mere mile of it, runs down again to the fields. But the view is gracious, and the air earns all the compliments that Shakespeare paid to the less deserving climate of sluggish Inverness. The land breeds pensive but not ungenial men whose philosophy has hard, clear lines. Boyhood turned honest farms into its land of fancy-free, made every trout a salmon, and every cushat a capercailzie ; other years see other things. It is not all loss.

All that has gone is quantity. Quality remains. No glory, save that of stature, has departed. Rather has glory increased. To go in search of one's youth is to have done with the nonsense preached with a sublime eloquence by Wordsworth in his *Ode on the Intimations of Immortality*. To grow up in body is to grow up in spirit. The eye develops with the frame, appreciation with the spread of limb. The shades of the prison house with which the poet threatened adolescence are indeed the fiction of brain-sickly brooding. Take the village. What was it to a boy but the goal of a morning journey ? There were lessons waiting in the study at the manse ; there was

toffee at the village-shop.   But now I can see that
village and praise the wisdom that built it under the
woods and above the burn, in as sweet a nook as
Scotland can contain.   I can praise the fitness of its
shaping, and see that the houses of native stone have
grown up like living things in perfect kinship with
their landscape.   The queer house that is half a fort-
ress, the manse that is at once kindly and formal like
a domesticated kirk, home of stern virtues and of
gentle flowers and fruit, the twist and surge of the
rambling street—all these were nothing then.   They
are much now.   My boyhood, at least, had no vision
splendid to surround its practical journeying.   It
thought of guns, fishing-rods, and sweetmeats.   It
breathed no larger air.

So there is good in growing up.   The boy cannot
see the wood for the trees, the burn for the lurking
trout, the moor for the possible excitements of beast
and bird.   Now beauty comes in, life's compensation
for adventure.   The compensation outweighs the loss.
The village takes its place in the scheme of things ;
it is the work of generations of living, labouring men.
Its crannied walls have the flowers which you may
search for the ultimate mysteries.   But the walls need
not drive you so far into the byways of reflection.
They have their more obvious story and are the testament of the grey, orderly, but not ungenial culture of
Eastern Scotland.   So, at the end of a sentimental
journey, one may bask without regrets.   Wonder has
gone, but admiration remains.   The meadow has lost
its mystery, but found its meaning, and takes its place
in a scheme of things far beyond the scope and range
of childish mind.   The black wood that housed Jack
Redskin no longer enfolds imaginary denizens.   Does
it matter ?   It is beautiful now as well as black.   The

house in which I gladly lived has become the house at which I gladly look. It is a generous exchange. It is indeed worth while to go in search of one's youth. That is dead and may not be discovered. But all the things that boyhood missed, how excellent they are !

From "Masques and Phases"

LONDON IN AUGUST

ALEC WAUGH

IT is over at last, the noise and hurry of July, and in obscure corners of Scotland and Brittany and Wales the exhausted Londoner is recovering from a succession, night after night, of dances and theatres and receptions. He is not sorry to be away. It has been great fun while it has lasted. But one can have too much of it. And, besides, London is impossible in August. There are few more melancholy spectacles than the litter of a room after the last guest has said " Good-bye," and what has London been for the last ten weeks but an immense incessant party ? When the band ceases let the dancing stop.

Impossible in August—that is what every one says of London. And the man who finds himself, for the first time, constrained to linger there during the unfashionable weeks indulges in an orgy of self-pity. " Isn't it perfectly appalling ? " he will tell his friends. " Do you know that I may have to stay in London the whole of August ? " " In London ? " they will reply, with that particular note of gratified commiseration which we reserve for our friends' misfortunes. " But, my dear fellow, what will you find to do there ? " And he will shrug his shoulders and wait with increasing dread for the closing of the first shutter across the windows of the square.

When the worst happens, however, when what was

probable has become a fact, when it is certain that no possible combination of circumstances can rescue him, he makes, as do the wise always, the best of a bad job. " I have got," he says, " to stay in this miserable town six miserable weeks. It is a tragedy —but there it is ! Nothing can be done about it. I must be content to make those weeks as tolerable as I can." And his first step is to discover which of his friends are victims of the same misfortune. His second to arrange a dinner-party. As is appropriate, he issues his invitations lugubriously. There will be a funeral feast, he says. Let them be the mourners. The corpse is to be interred decently on the second Wednesday of the month.

The ritual of the interment is, he finds, however, considerably more enlivening than he had expected.

The restaurant is pleasantly empty. The waiter has time in plenty to discuss, in such manner as waiters should, the distinctive natures of the various wines upon his list. There is no hurry. No one has to rush off at half-past nine " to collect a partner." And how many such parties have not, during the past season, been ruined by that excuse ?

Slowly, tranquilly, the evening passes. And as they rise from the table it is agreed generally that there must be a repeat performance. " On Friday," says one of them, " you will come, all of you, and dine with me. If it's as warm as it is to-day, we'll eat out in the garden." And so, two days later, they sit and talk quietly, while the air cools slowly and the pale greens of the sky darken, and there is about them a stillness and tranquillity they did not know that London had for giving.

Every place and every season has its own qualities, its particular properties that are to be found nowhere

else.   And London has to give us in August something
that it can give us at no other time.   For nine-tenths
of the year London life, with its noise and colour and
animation, is like a story by Dostoieffsky.   In August
it is like a story by Turgenev, still and calm and deep.

In London we meet too many people to be intimate
with more than a very few.   And during the rush of
a crowded season we neither see our old friends nor
make new ones.   We live in an eternal atmosphere
of acquaintanceship, and acquaintanceship stands in
the same relationship to friendship that a flirtation
does to a love affair—exciting but unsatisfying.   A
man who is just passing out of middle age told me
the other day that, more than anything else, he regretted the number of acquaintanceships in his life
that had never developed into friendships—acquaintanceships that would have so developed had the
setting for them been different.   " Friendships," he
added, " do not flower easily in London."

We recognize delightedly a familiar face among a
pack of strangers.   There is an effusive welcome.
How splendid that we should meet !   How well we
are looking !   Have we been to Ascot ?   Are we
going to Lords ?   What has happened to So-and-so ?
We maintain for five minutes a fusillade of animated
chatter.   And then we realize that we are both
searching the noise beyond for some face we know.
" Oh, but there's So-and-so," we say ;   " I must just
go and speak to him."

That is what is always happening.   Friendship
needs leisure for its setting.   And there is little of that
in London.   It may sound a paradox, but it is a fact
that we have in June and July scarcely enough vitality
to sustain a quiet evening.   We have to keep ourselves
on a highly geared and artificial level of animation

if we are to forget that we have been dancing half the night, that if we were left alone for two minutes we should be asleep.

And that is why certain of us, while the rest of the world are packing trunks and delving into time-tables, are arranging contentedly among ourselves for a month of quiet evenings. One would not, of course, always like London to be like that. By the beginning of October there will begin to return the old itch for dancing and noise and varied company. But for six weeks of the fifty-two to have London so. . . . My only fear is that too many people may discover how extraordinarily pleasant it can be.

From " On Doing What One Likes "

A WAR SPRING IN HYDE PARK

JAMES MILNE

What the eye saw, and missed, when even Nature was being squeezed for the sinews of battle, when the gardeners had all gone with the Colours, and the Call of the Wild was asserting itself in the finest demesne of our bravely respondent London Town.

When spring unlocks the flowers, to paint the laughing soil.
Seventh Sunday after Trinity

The soote [sweet] season, that bud and bloom forth brings
When grene hath clad the hill, and eke the vale.
HENRY HOWARD, EARL OF SURREY

SPRING is moving in Hyde Park, but it is the second spring of the Great War, and it is not like other springs. The poets, if there are any of them left from the War, to take up the lyre of Nature, will have to write special odes for this spring. Possibly they will not be inspired, because some of the inspiring things are absent, but that would be a pity. It would be a pity to miss their sonnets, for sonnets are always well intentioned, even if we must miss most of the flowers which were gorgeous in Hyde Park.

You may take your walk there now, but whether it rains or blusters snow, or is sunshine, you will not see the budding flower-pots of peace days. The economy of War-time has laid its hand upon the flowers of Hyde Park, and they do not laugh at you, and nod to you, and beckon you with their gay motions, as they did a year ago. A cold stroke of saving, wielded by an institution called the Office of Works, has passed over them, and they lie buried under the soil, or, rather, they are not there at all.

No, there has not, in these recent months, been the planting of roots and the bedding-out of them that there used to be, with the consequence that Hyde Park looks plain, as if, somehow, it had been shaved bare by the winter winds. The grass is green and fresh and spring-like, but where are the clusters of maiden blooms that used to bow and bend to each other in the early spring wind, sweet fairies come out of the dark recesses of the earth ? You cannot see them, because, like the Spanish fleet of the Elizabethan age, they are not yet in sight, and, unlike it, they are not going to come in sight.

Nothing, not even a great war, can take from us the spacious, splendid acres of Hyde Park, the finest park in the world. Nothing can take from us the Serpentine, and the Long Water, away beyond it in Kensington Gardens, over the bridge, where the sun sets red in the west and the March clouds are cold and angry. Nothing can steal from us the splendid avenue of trees which borders Rotten Row, nor the whole rich arborage that raises a kindly, green roof over the greener glades below. Hyde Park is inalienable, but the hand of the gardener is niggardly with it, and its dells without a name will have to make up for those little gardens which used to give it the colours of the hyacinth, the daffodil, the tulip, the lily, and the brazen rhododendron.

It was a riot of colour which met you, from the statue of Achilles away up to the foot of the Serpentine. This spring you will have to see that riot in fancy, because you will not see it in fact. You will miss it, but possibly you will agree that plainness goes naturally with the War-time, and, at all events, you will try to find in that argument a solace for the absent colour. And yet, and yet, you will be sorry and unconvinced, wondering if flower-beds which gave Londoners so much joy might not have bloomed on.

There will be flowers, not, maybe, the ordered plots of luxuriant colours born and nurtured in hothouses, but the wild blossoms that spring up through glade and grass, indifferent whether there be war or peace upon the earth. Nay, not indifferent, because those wild flowers have been Nature's comforters to the eye ever since the world began, and it will be sweet to look for them and find them and make much of them, especially as they have been a little overlooked in the presence of their more gorgeous fellows, tended by all the arts of the gardener.

You will find bluebells in Hyde Park if you know where to look for them, and if you know the way to look at them you will see how pleased they are with your coming, how they nod and laugh to each other in your presence, thinking it flattery. Yes, the wild flowers of Hyde Park are going to have a very great time in the Great War, and if you are wise you will go forth and let them share it with you.

From "A New Tale of Two Cities"

SEPTEMBERITIS

R. S. HOOPER

SEPTEMBER is rather a sad month in some ways. It reminds me of spinsterhood, that dangerous age between missing opportunities and abandoned hope. It's neither one thing nor the other. Generally the sun shines after a moist July and a torrential August, and shines too late. The leaf is turning ; the dews are rising ; the evenings, as we are never tired of remarking in any company, are beginning to draw in. With the exception of an uncomfortably hot May and a brief spell of warmth in June, we have had no summer, and this has happened almost since time immemorial. No one expects August to be fine, and July is written down by most people as a thoroughly unreliable month. I believe if we made up our minds never to take our holidays in July and August we should cease to be a cold-blooded race. Perhaps it's just as well we don't. I know several cold-blooded people well enough to tremble at the thought of what they'd be like if something took the chill off their circulation. But September. . . . It is wearing on. Soon it will be October. I don't like it.

There are several of life's lesser problems that engage my inner self at this time of the year. They loom all the larger because of the first feeling of autumn in the air. It is subconsciously depressing. I met a man to-day, for instance, with his first winter

cold. He talked to me with glistening eyes, and
trumpeted between the sentences. I backed away
from him, and left him murmuring something about
whisky and aspirins. You could have seen his nose
in the dark. Only yesterday I played my last game
of tennis. I hoped it was the last, because my form
always disappears at the end of the summer, and if
the season went on much longer people would begin
to ask me to come late and leave my racquet behind.

All the same, though the light is impossible, the
wind too high, and the balls too tired, it is a sad
thought that you have served your last double fault
and said your last " Sorry." One tries so pitifully
hard to pretend it's still summer. " Isn't it wonderful to be playing at this time of year ? " some one
says, buttoning up a woolly waistcoat, and wondering
if anyone would mind if he played in gloves. After
tea the breeze freshens, and long shadows fall across
the court. The sun slips quietly down behind the
herbaceous border, and a girl in white, with a nose
turning a faint imperial purple, lobs into the teeth of
the gale, and thinks gloomily of the long winter
evenings with her mother.

Meanwhile, my partner tells me we've won the
toss, and begs me to serve against the wind before
we change over and get the sun, or rather the herbaceous border, in our eyes. He says my deliveries
when the breeze has finished with them are untakable,
whereas with the wind behind them there is no need
to take them at all. I blow on my hands, and the
last game of the year begins. One by one the on-
lookers collect their wraps and say their good-byes.
I envy them as they depart in search of a hot bath
and, with luck, a log fire after dinner. How dark it
is all of a sudden. Look, there's a bat. It is coming

towards me. No, it isn't a bat ; it's a black plum.
The wind has blown it from the tree. It is a wind-
fall. Now it's getting bigger . . . some plum. . . . I
shall keep the stone and weigh it . . . how bad the
light is . . . it is coming nearer . . . perhaps it is a
tennis ball . . . it must be. . . . I will strike it. . . .
I have struck it . . . it is gone. Yes, I think so . . . in
the third clump. Behind the agapanthus. I marked
it most carefully. Fifteen-forty. . . . Love-four you
lead. Anybody's game. . . . Sorry, partner.

Next time the white trousers come back from the
wash their fate will be a deep drawer and the cam-
phor balls. It is a melancholy business putting them
away, worse than saying good-bye to your dormouse
before it retires into its winter sleep.

People will soon be asking me what I think of the
autumn tints, and I shall say they are the most
wonderful I have ever seen. I've never known an
autumn when the tints weren't better than last year.
Either that or there aren't any tints at all. I once
wrote a poem about them called *Golden Leaves*, a
sad, moaning little thing with a wonderful last verse
which would have been better still if I could have
found a rhyme to ' russet.' The only one I know
is a worse word than placket. I recited the poem to
my mother when she had rheumatism, and, if I remember right, she cried. Mothers are so easily
moved. She said when she looked through the window, and saw the rain and the falling leaves, that a
shiver ran right through her. I said it was the cold
touch of Winter's finger laying the mute ghost of
Spring. But the doctor thought it was rheumatism.

I suppose an optimist would call September the
best month of the year. He would draw your attention to the apples and tell you that the sunshine was

M

mellow. He would urge you to take your summer gladly, however late it came, and babble hopefully of a good old-fashioned winter and a wonderful spring. But soon the words will be sticking in his throat. The sun will go in and stay in, and there won't be anything old-fashioned about the winter. Weather permitting, it will be one of those modern muggy affairs with a steady drizzle and another epidemic of influenza.

But before the worst happens there comes that uncomfortable interregnum which produces in my system the disease called " Septemberitis." It comes primarily from pretending the sun is hot when it is only mellow. This delusion results in the dangerous prolongation of the period of thin shirts and summer suits. After a week's acute discomfort I put on a flannel shirt, and make myself feel warmer by promising to get out all my winter wardrobe if it gets any colder. One morning it is so cold that I go the whole hog, and plunge into long woollen things that tickle, and the second best of my two winter suits. Next day all is mellow again, and after enduring tortures of apoplexy I finish up the evening in my shirt-sleeves and a thorough draught. The day after brings a slight chill and the beginning of the first cold snap. Not expecting it, I have gone back to a cotton shirt and taken the hatguard off my boater. Result : east wind on the liver, spots before the eyes, a hot-water bottle, chilblains, and, if one isn't careful, a quiet gathering at the crematorium with no flowers at 2 p.m. Nearest tube station Golders Green ; hymn No. 21 in the old books.

I suppose one might get over the difficulty by ordering a succession of suits of all textures and not getting up till lunch-time. By then the early morn-

ing mists would have cleared off, and you could tell
more or less what sort of a day you were in for.
Personally, finding it impossible to do either, I must
choose between freezing and suffocation, or else pro-
ceed to the duties of the day with two shirts, prepared
to remove the outer one at the first sign of St Luke's
summer.   Some people prefer to wear two detachable
waistcoats, or spend the day indoors with an overcoat.
Women, of course, with expensive fur coats hardly
ever take them off at all.   I've seen them on a warm
September evening sweltering in the stalls covered in
mink or beaver, and hoping that the fur-less woman
behind is turning a bilious green with envy.

Very soon, to add to one's forebodings, comes the
thought of the first fire.   For days you struggle
against it, but in the end it is bound to come.   After
a few nights of going to bed early and leaving it unlit,
some one, greatly daring, produces a match and sets
fire to a piece of newspaper.   The excitement then
becomes intense.   A dare-devil feeling of affluence
steals over the owner of the fourteen lumps of coal
and the well-seasoned faggots.   A little smoke rises
from the back page of the *Daily Mail* and drifts out
into the room.   Somebody picks up the bellows and
blows it back again.   One stick splutters, turns red,
then black, and smoulders gently.   If everybody has
finished with to-day's paper the expert fire-lighter
volunteers to put matters right.   More matches, more
bellows, and the first fire is hissing and cracking.
Draw the curtains, pull up your chairs, turn on the
light, and let us get on with the winter.   And by all
means let us forget the price of coal and the prospect
of being disturbed in an hour's time to eat cold beef
in a stone-cold dining-room.

I have begun to notice the draughts now, and other

things about the house, like open windows and chill-some passages.   One day there will occur that painful ceremony of dividing up the remainder of this year's tennis balls between the dog and the children.   Next year I shall want another new racquet and a further supply of flannels.   Worked out in an equivalent of therms or tons of coal, the cost is going to be un-thinkable.   Some one (not me) will probably want a new fur coat.   I wonder if she'll get it ?   I don't want to be gloomy, but these thoughts crowd in upon one so in September.

By the way, have you noticed how quickly the evenings . . .

I said it first.

From "One at a Time"

OCTOBER TREES AND FLOWERS

H. J. MASSINGHAM

IN the early days of a quiet October, the sun soon makes a mouthful of the morning mist, and the tops of the woods are still Quakerish in hue. Summer pushes its brown-suited forces deep into the homelands of autumn.

By mid-October, if the weather has not broken, the four seasons make a kind of composite revelry before life finally ebbs into the lassitude of winter and leaves the world to the passions of the elements. Brown, green, and fiery leaves, naked twigs, packed buds, and sun-stained fruits are all displayed upon one plant, like the shelf of an untidy bibliophile of a general taste. The sallows in the hedgerows and thickets are studded with the silvery ' palm ' catkins in their yellowish-green sheaths, climbing every branchlet, while most of the hazels swing theirs.

Trees turn their coats slowly or quickly according to their organic constitution, their sheltered or open position, the richness or poverty, moisture or aridity of the soil, as well as according to the rhythm of the seasons. The most conspicuous trees in the landscape of the home counties are the ashes, whose uniform lemon-yellow or pale gold leaves are illuminated to their full value by the dark purple of the branches against the azure sky, and shine with an evening light. Some are hung with nut-brown samaras (the ' keys ' or ' spinners '—the sail has a twist which spins

the ' key ' away on the wind and brings it to earth
with the seed-end on the ground) ; some in full
summer foliage, while others are fired in numerous
small patches. Gilpin called the ash the " Venus of
the Woods," and this refined gold has a queenly distinction which makes the yellow of the maples look
even dirtier than it is.

Many of the deeply veined leaves of the dogwood
persist in green, and shoot their cymes of creamy
flowers above the hedgetops, though the usual flowering time is June and July. When red stems (an old
English name of the dogwood is the goad-bush), rich
coppery-red leaves, flowers and darkly flushed berries
are mingled in the hedge, the effect is of a confusing
brilliance. The ivy is in flower and in fruit, and the
immature male catkins of the alders (darker than the
hazel catkin), the full cones, and the empty black
ones, all spread simultaneously, deepen the impression
of October as the junction of the seasons.

Those plebeian plants, the purging and breaking
buckthorns, also help to telescope summer and
autumn. Breaking might well be called the scowling
buckthorn, and the dark, sour-looking leaves accom-
pany a multitude of buds, while purging buckthorn,
which is less forbidding in appearance for all its
spines, sheds its yellowish-green leaves for the worms
to inter. In a fine October it is the golden-brown
buds of the beech rather than the yellowing leaves
that glitter in the sun, and the bloom is still on the
year, as at the base of many a fallen acorn purpling
the brown. Upon the juniper there is a double
bloom, that of the purple berries and the soft glaucous
sheen of the upper sides of the leaves, differing from
that of the silver fir, whose leaf, also shaped like a
cobbler's awl, is banded by silver on either side of

the midrib, on the under side. The Lombardy poplars are discrowned, and serve as a chapel for the evening ritual-songs of the starlings, but some of the holly berries are still unripe, and the dark polished leaves of the bay hide scarlet and purple berries which sometimes touch.

The twinkling leaves of the aspen are an expressive symbol of the mobile face of the English landscape, with its delicate texture and ephemeral moods. When green, brown, and yellow leaves catch the high lights on the same branchlet, and the sticky buds point from the axils, it seems to represent the mazy dance of spring, summer, and autumn.

The unkept hedgerows as yet betray none of the wreckage of the declining year, but the leaves of way-side trees come sailing down upon them. They glide past the panoply of plumpy hip and haw, dogwood berries of the hue of dragon's blood, scarlet berries of the two bryonies and the arum in the lee of the hedges, the purplish-black clusters of sloe and privet berries, shining like boot-buttons, the carmine berries of the yew with a rosier tinge in the spindle-tree, and the tufted, filmy plumelets of traveller's joy, which Gerarde turned from silver into gold by naming it. October is hung with beads and earrings and em-broidery, like a gipsy maid. And I can look along a distant hedgerow and see green followed by golden yellow, then apple-green and burnt sienna to come after—the coat of our dormouse, fox, and squirrel, the breast of our robin, the mantle of our butcher-birds. Dark green looms behind that, and so the pictured story runs with variations of pink and purple, harmonies of different colours in the same key.

But in the home counties flowers are not so easy to

find, and they are the stragglers of vanished hosts.
Here and there they live in gay unmindfulness, hemp
nettle and marjoram along the hedges and forget-
me-not along the brooks, tiny red splashes of pim-
pernel in the stubble by the woodside, a party of
centaury playing at summer in the shelter of the
junipers on the chalk slopes, and field scabious at the
edges of the pastures, still honoured by the bee.   But
others bloom in the graveyards of their own dead,
and a Canterbury bell lives touching his withered
brother on the same stalk.   On the common a chance
harebell hides its azure under a sombre gorse-bush,
like Mariana in the moated grange, a head of ragwort flares, the last flicker of summer fires, with here
and there a stray candle-flame from the gorse itself.
Come storm, and all the brave fabric of life tumbles
and the year is in ruins.

" West," is what my pulse beats in October, and
the migratory impulse is hot upon me to flee the
cold, the wind, the dark, and the rain before the
shouting mob comes to tear autumn royalty to rags.
Cold numbs my brain and my feelings even more
than my body, and the Methodist east wind rushes
upon me, an East Anglian without a drop of other
blood in my veins, with the withering force of old
age.

What joy it is to me to ramble the flowery autumn
fields of Somerset and Dorset and feel that as the
warm living year goes out I for a brief while am
dogging its footsteps ! To count the flowers on
Dorset heath, pasture, down, or cliff-edge is not for
me a cataloguer's pride, but a sort of bead-telling in
sun-worship, and I love flowers, not only for their
own sakes in differing degrees of beauty and for their
personal appeal or association, but because they are

the breath and language of " bright Phœbus in his
strength," who is hardly less desirable to me than to
frisking lizard and sluggish adder.

I have sometimes wondered whether this primitive,
heathen, instinctive sun-need had anything to do with
a strange experience I had in October while lying in
the circular trench of a British round barrow, pre-
Keltic by a thousand years, lonely among the high
Downs and overlooking grim, disembowelled Portland
Bill. It was the smallest barrow I had ever seen even
in that county so thick with the grassy tumuli of the
dead which haunt the roads of the Roman con-
querors, and was in strong contrast to the massive
citadel of Mai Dun, a few miles away. It was protected from the upland winds by a small plantation
of beech, whose leaves, owing to the exposure of the
stunted trees, had already fallen or clung lifeless to
the writhen branches.

It was a place on which the years had made no
more impression than had the footsteps of passing
beetles, and it throbbed not with the ghosts but the
voices of the Iberian Roundheads, and of those who
displaced but were mingled with them, small and
fierce and restless like human *felidæ*. Incessantly they
whispered to one another among the trees, now low
and furtively, now eagerly and furiously in a gathering,
hissing storm of anger and fear. They talked like
beech-leaves in the wind, and it was so I felt it with
an incommunicable vividness and reality. It was, of
course, the inviolable remoteness and associations of
the place which obliterated the measurements of time,
but I think that the wintriness of the trees in the
midst of a nature ripe and plumped with increase
and gay with beads strung over her brilliant dress
may have helped by the shock of contrast to make

the mind receptive to the contiguity of these ancient dead.[1]

But to the flowers. Bluebells are the spring skies of earth, and the stems of spring plants seem to tether to the soil flowers more rightly ether's. But the flowers of autumn are the excellence of the labour of earth, and for woodland skies there are purple mists in the open fields. Devil's bit scabious, with its rich violet centre is what chiefly paints them so. Gerarde, to whom flowers were a kind of Society for the Promotion of Happiness, because he esteemed them for their beauty as well as their properties, says of it : " Old fantasticke charmers report that the Devil did bite it for envie because it is an herbe that hath so many good virtues." Are the modern botanists freer of old wives' tales when they name the proudest of the knapweeds, that common aristocrat of October and the hedgeside, whose florets radiate outwards in sweeping lines and curves like antlers—*Centaurea scabiosa*—because Chiron used it in his healing art? The devil's bit hath the good virtue of matching the full, deep tones of the year's closing journey, as the bluebell suggests the imparadised mystery of spring.

At a distance the field is uniform purple, but wade through it and it is as variegated as a hedgerow.

[1] The long barrows were earlier and raised by the Longheads who built the great Avebury cromlech centuries before Stonehenge, the work of the Roundheads, who, it seems, had a civilization something akin to the Aztec before the Spaniards came. Arnold's " the dark Iberians came, And on the shore undid their corded bales " must be a mistake, for the first Iberians, according to modern views, crossed over to England before it was separated from the Continent. They were the Azilians, who broke up the Cro-Magnon civilization at the final retreat of the glaciers. Arnold perhaps meant the Phœnicians of Carthage. Some say an Alpine race invaded the Iberians of Britain and in their turn were conquered by the Kelts about 500 B.C. On the other hand, the Cretans were also great seamen, and they were Iberians.

Betony (the old Saxon bishopswort and a salve against elf-disease and demoniacal possession), single heads of flax, the minute lilac-coloured field madder with its narrow, pointed leaves like a starfish, the long-stalked, waving *Geranium columbinium*, purple with a rosy tinge and delicate as the harebell, the purple variety of the heartsease, and other flowers break up the purple sheet into different shades and travel into blues and lavenders.

Of the blues, the richest and most autumnal are those of borage and succory. Bugloss, says Gerarde of another borage, hath a virtue " to drive away sorrow and pensiveness and to comfort and strengthen the heart." But I prefer the cerulean blue of the common borage, with its clustered purplish-black stamens protruding from the centre, a blue worthy to be compared with the blues of the gentians and into whose little firmament the mind is lifted above all cloudiness and heaviness. In the seventeenth century still-room books there is a return to the belief in the influences of herbs upon the heavenly bodies, and two centuries later the belief had another re-incarnation : " Thou canst not touch a flower without troubling of a star " :

> Linking such heights and such humilities
> That I do think my tread,
> Stirring the blossoms in the meadow-grass,
> Flickers the unwithering stars.

One's lion liberty may range at will in the heavenly fields of borage blue.

The blue of succory at the field's edge, a large sessile flower with coarsely toothed leaves like the dandelion's, is much paler. But it has the peculiar quality of being at the same time rich and intense, intense with the passion of the moment rather than in depth, like borage and gentian blue, and it is this gives it a special distinction.

For the complementary yellows to these blues, there were the dull yellow of fennel, the bright and limpid yellows of St John's wort and meadow vetchling and eyebright touched in the centre with the tenderest yellow of all. Myth said the eyebright was a cure for heartache, science names it *Euphrasia*, semi-parasite as it is, and it looks fit for an angel's button-hole, so that the truth is one, only there are different ways of putting it. Red bartsia, the lichen-coloured seeded heads of wild carrot, like a goldfinch's nest, and humbler flowers, such as the cudweed with its curiously worked effect of blended greys, browns, and silvers, the rosy clusters of the slender polygonum, and the farthing dips of the insignificant white crucifer, penny cress with its broad-winged pods—these were the varicoloured freshets and eddies in the purple lake. But the sceptre of the fields was lady's tresses, with its worthy Latin name of *Spiranthes autumnalis*. It is an orchid, and the greenish-white flowers wind close round the stem up to its tip in a lovely spiral, blos-soming as they climb. Does it appear like a wreathed spire to the beetle clambering among the grass stalks ?

I love to see October pile up her wealth like a floral millionaire,

> to set budding more
> And still more, later flowers for the bees,
> Until they think warm days will never cease,
> For Summer has o'erbrimm'd their clammy cells;

and if that be a vulgar, early-Marlowesque desire, it is because I can see winter, that desert anchorite, advancing upon our golden revels. I shall not then easily forget an untended beet-field on the edge of Studland cliffs gone agriculturally rusty with " the weeds as you call them," [1] a fair of them encamped in mobs upon it. " Brave flowers, that I might gallant it like you ! " my thought was as I stood in an acre of corn marigolds. The pleasant old writer, Bartolomæus Anglicus, remarks of them that they draw evil humours out of the head and strengthen the eyesight. Who hath stood among a treasure trove of these infant suns cannot doubt it. In form they are the suns in old engravings, and in blaze they are the true sun-colour, and of a flaming splendour against the sea's blue. I gathered an armful of them, as though I were raking in my gambling gains over the green table.

And foaming and trailing in dense tufts and fantastic loops among the stems of the marigolds was heaped the smooth, fine, glaucous foliage of the fumitory with its racemes of flowers in varying shades from vinous to rose-madder, like a waggon-load of embroidery dropped and left on the ground, to make lace collars for the marigolds. There were the white campion and the spike of the small-flowered Silene like a minute campion with petals red and white and fair enough, and poppies and the slender vetch pale blue and the earlier common vetch with reddish-purple leaves. The lesser snapdragon was not to be overlooked, and threw out its slender leaves and cupped its smaller flowers in long fingers yet more slender.

Spurges no less than vetches made common ground, the sun spurge and the petty spurge with their little flower-heads wrapped up in the bracts and laid upon a platter of oval leaves, like chocolates in their frills set out upon a dish. But how tell them apart, except

[1] Coles in *The Art of Simpling*. See Miss Rohde's *Old English Herbals*.

that the petty spurge looks of a flimsier make, and the leaves of the sun spurge are of a golden green? The secret is that the involucral glands of the *petty* spurge are . . .

I should turn the bright wealth of this October field into a column of dull figures, if I were to count it all up, and but three more will I mention—the musk erodium, because of its musky smell and the quaint length of the stork's bills set upright at the ends of their peduncles like Christmas-tree candles, the corn sow-thistle, because it is a much finer plant than either common or marsh sow-thistle and has a big inflorescence of magnificent shining yellow, like the sun of another planet drifted among the marigolds, and lastly the uncommon annual mercury. The delicate greenish florets (males) are borne on spikes of much the same length as the almost transparent leaves, and both rise diagonally from the nodes of the stem, so that flowers and leaves are mingled into a handsome design, like a Grinling Gibbons carving.

I must leave the many fine October flowers of the Dorset Downs (which are like no other Downs in the world, no, not even the loud-sung Downs of Sussex). The *Senecio squalidus*, which has no English name, and is more open-flowered than the common ragwort ; the leafless meadow saffron, a spiritualized crocus ; the delicate perfoliate yellow-wort, which has its own share of the distinction and originality of the gentians, and the Carline thistle which lacks the charm of Clare's spear-thistle or of the spreading crinolines of the dwarf-thistle and the humble nobility of the bowed head of the musk-thistle, but is individual in having its seed-heads coloured a beautiful raw umber for the usual thistle white. And there are many others.

But one loves best the flowers that grow in soil more personal and intimate than other soils with other flowers more fair, and so I will end with a few of October's gaieties upon the prehistoric, twilight heaths and bogs, heedless of the mouse-like scratchings of time, beneath whose mere, once an arm of the sea, Excalibur lies buried.

There is a story that Linnæus fell on his knees before the blossoming furze on Putney Heath and thanked God for creating a plant so lovely. But even when their bushes are burning out and bell heather, ling, and cross-leaved heath with rosy top-knots are going brown, there are many happy pipes and flutes breaking in here and there to tune with the deep ancestral undertones of the heath.

One of them is the little composite flower, the saw-wort (named from the serrated leaves) whose pistil is horned and whose florets are tinged with faint purple. But the nicest thing about it is a trellised calyx, as though nature were loth we should miss so pretty but small a member of so large a family, and carved this ornament to call our attention. The pinkish lousewort is a sufferer with the squinancy-wort, but the hood arches over the three-lobed underlip and makes an effect to vindicate the flower's innocence. The more happily named labiate, the lesser skullcap, occupies the more boggy ground, and with the protruded lower lip spotted with crimson seems to declare with a flourish and write it down in blood that by no means is it a smaller cousin of the lousewort, as it looks. The sundews [1] of the peat bog were back in the summer, though their dewy glands still glistened invitingly. The humming-bird of the

[1] *Drosera rotundifolia* and *anglica* were the species, the rarer *anglica* with larger flowers and much narrower leaves.

heath, the tiny milkwort " fashioned like a little bird, with wings, tail and body," whose six varieties of colour Gerarde faithfully chronicled, ran into a laughing blue upon the sandy waste, and from the black water still rose scattered spikes of the buckbean, radiantly white, like a naiad bathing.

The buckbean or marsh trefoil, so called from its design of three oval leaves upon a leaf-stalk, is of the gentian family, and the gentians might well form the coronet of October, since of the five species of the genus *Gentiana*, four open their calm, classic beauty to the autumn. One of these, the rare marsh gentian, grew in profusion among the grey and golden lichens in the drier portions of the bog, at the foot of the great rock which the Devil in one of his boisterous moods threw at Corfe Castle from the Isle of Wight, and missed. It carries its long blue vase at the end of the fragile stem and looks gravely into the blue sky. The corolla is outwardly striped with five green ribbons, and the spotted rims of the petals are lit with a faint violet glow. I can think of no other term for the marsh gentian's intense, still, dreamlike hue than to call it a devotional blue, and to that the statuesque appearance of the plant lends support. It usually bore but one flower, but sometimes two and rarely three, and there was one plant pure white, tipped with faint grey-green spots, and at the bottom of the tube reposed a minute orange spider.

But the blue flowers were the most beautiful, and everywhere about them grew the golden-orange spikes of withered bog-asphodel. Crimson and gold, scarlet and purple are the insignia of October, and here in orange and blue was a new combination for the month placed between fulfilment and the promise of spring. It seemed to me to give just the right note of October's mingled richness and spirituality, to show them in harmony, and to rid the prejudiced human mind of its bent to associate the ascetic with the spiritual. Heaven is nothing to us without the warmth and dearness of earth.

From "Untrodden Ways"

N

AS YOU LIKE IT

LIKES AND DISLIKES

JAMES AGATE

THESE are my likings.

An old park in our middle England, dripping trees, undergrowth, decay, a lady many years disconsolate ; bleak, pinched moors and winding roads ; old inns, coffee-rooms, and faded prints ; high noon in market-squares, the roguery of dealers, Hodge's reverence to parson and bank manager ; all that England which lies between Hogarth and Trollope ; the placidity which is content with Rydal Water and the glory of Wordsworth ; the eaves and thatches of Hertfordshire ; Surrey's imitation of Corot ; the apple-sense of Somerset ; the mothy coombes of Devon. And then the reflex sentimentality of these direct emotions and the play Stevenson would have made of them ; the Wardour Street glamour of such words as ' sun-dial ' and ' curfew,' the Victorian lilt and cadence of that perfect *raseur* King Arthur ; the saturated melancholy of headstones. The sentimentality of parchments ; old brocades, fans that have not fluttered and lace that has not stirred for a generation ; the *mouches* and petulance of *petites marquises* ; the painter's sense of great ladies.

I could tease myself that these emotions are so general as not to be worth the setting down, were it not that strong affection loses nothing by being shared with the whole world. Sealing-wax and sailing-ships

fascinate me none the less for having appealed to
another. Yet there are certain intimate apprecia-
tions, discoveries of one's own, to be hugged exult-
ingly. Such the homely lilt of ballads, the crinolined
grace of *She wore a Wreath of Roses*, the faded propriety
of *My Mother bids me bind my Hair*. I sometimes think
they have missed the better half of life who do not
know Claribel, stern mistress of our tender youth,
inexorable guide to wayward fingers. Well do I
remember the tone of ivory keys deepening through
saffron to rich brown, the nubbly, polished ebonies,
the puckered rose-coloured silk lining, the fretted
walnut front, the fantastic scroll-work of the maker's
name. Collard and Collard—how many hours did
my childish soul ponder over all the possible com-
binations of father and son, uncle and nephew,
brothers it may be. I often find myself wondering
what has become of the old piano over which half
my childhood was wept away. I believe I should
know it again by its fragrance, the fragrance of my
mother's fingers. As I write the perfume steals across
me.

I adore all acting, all masks and subterfuges, all
cloaks and garbs of respectability, the obsequiousness
of head waiters and the civility of underlings, all
rogues and vagabonds soever, the leer of the pavement and the wit of the gutter. I love Bond Street
at eleven in the morning, Scott's at noon, some
matinée at which there shall be question of faded
emotion—say, the old retainer's. And then sunset,
red as a guardsman's tunic, gilding the front of the
westward-going bus, a music-hall, enough money in
my pocket to pay the small-hours' supper bill, the
lights extinguished and by the butt of a glowing cigar,
a last florin for its fellow, a last sixpence for human

débris insistent with pitiful whine. I love the mystery and peril of the streets. I love to lie lazily in London, to loop my curtains and surrender myself to the hypnotic effect of the one hundred and sixty-three stags and two thousand two hundred and eighty-two hounds in full cry which I must presume to have been my landlord's taste in wall-paper some lustres ago. I like to gaze at framed elevens and fifteens, at the jumble of racquets and clubs, the jowl of a prize-fighter, Vardon at the top of his swing, Miss Letty Lind ineffably graceful in some Chinese fantasy. I like to look down on Regent Street—my rooms are at the top of a nest of actors' clubs, registry offices, shady money-lenders, and still shadier solicitors—and watch the late last loiterer. I love to lie and think of the world as my own, my very own, in which, though I earn a living by rule and in tune with the common whim, I may by the grace of God think what I like and choose the friends who shall make me laugh and the books which shall make me cry. Every man leads a double life in this most precious of senses. In this world of my own I am supreme lord and master, and may shatter and rebuild according to my proper desire. Events in the tangible universe do not as events interest me at all. Kings may die and empires fade away, but until these happenings are presented in some saturated phrase my conscious-ness is unaffected. A new planet is of less moment to me than a new reading of an old line. It needed the Shakespearean echo of some journalist's " Now is England to be tested to her very marrow " to move me to the full responsibility of our pledge to Belgium.

I love the vanity of artists stretching their sad fasti-diousness on the rack till perfection be found ; the martyr's egotism which will sacrifice health and life

itself, not that we may read, but that he may write.
So the pride of the soldier, caring less for the cause
than that he shall die worthily. I love words for their
own sake. I love the words ' hyacinth,' ' narcissus,'
' daffodil,' ' dog-rose ' ; their very look on the page
enchants me ; they smell more sweetly in the writer's
garden than in Nature's rank parterre. I have never
seen a trumpet-orchid, yet I know that when I read :

> Fly forward, O my heart, from the Foreland to the Start—
>   We're steaming all too slow,
> And it's twenty thousand mile to our little lazy isle
>   Where the trumpet-orchids blow,

the word conjures up the nostalgia of far-off seas.
I love the tinkle of ' onyx,' ' chalcedony,' ' beryl,'
more than the trumpery gauds themselves. I love
the word ' must-stained ' without desire to gaze upon
the feet of the treader of grapes ; the words ' spike-
nard ' and ' alabaster ' without longing for pot or jar.
I am crazy for ' jasmine ' and for ' jade,' and were I
a French writer you would find *jadis* on every page.
I would give the million I do not possess to flaunt a
scutcheon with the device *Désormais !* But if I am in
love with words, it must not be supposed that I have
no affection for the idea also. Though I would insist
that the idea shall emerge from the foam and tumble
of its wrappings glorious as any goddess from the sea,
yet do I not disdain to disentangle the writer from
his own enmeshings, to lie in wait for him, to detect
him in his style. I like to hear in the slipshod cadence
of Dickens the beating of his great untidy heart ; to
trace in the lowering of beautiful words to unromantic
purpose the infinite common sense of his latter-day
successor ; to nose the corruption of the decadent in
the paint and powder of his prose. Words for me are
not the grace-notes of existence, but the very stuff

and texture of life. This may be madness, but it is
an honest frenzy, and remember that in your own
kingdom you have the right to be mad. I like to
think of Piccadilly as it must have been in those early
days which saw me mewed up in our provinces of
sterling worth. Of the *coudoiement* of notabilities. Of
the days when Ellen Terry brought a new morning
to the jaded world and Irving sent us shuddering to
bed ; when, touchingly, at eleven-thirty, Mr and Mrs
Kendal would make it up again. When Mr Beerbohm Tree was a rising actor and Mr George Moore
confesses he was young. When those tremendous
initials G. B. S. first growled and thundered in the
pages of *The Saturday Review*, Wilde had not tired of
confounding peacockery with prose, and the giant
Wells was stirring in his sleep. When Rudyard
Kipling was a power in the land, Lord Rosebery a
Liberal-Imperialist hope, and it seemed as though the
Prince would never be King.

I am a good lover, but an even better hater. I
have an unparalleled zest for the most moderate of
dislikes. I mislike—to put it no more strongly—a
great many women and nearly all men, with a special
aversion for the type of man adored by women,
mincing-mouthed, luxuriant-polled, *genre coiffeur*. I
mislike the purist who claims that one language should
be enough for any writer and secretly begrudges
Cæsar his dying Latinism ; and I mislike all those
honest folk who insist upon taking you at the foot of
the letter instead of at the top, or at least half-way
down. I dislike all aldermen, mayors, beadles,
janitors, pew-openers, the whole bag of officialdom ;
all sham repentances and most sincere ones ; all those
to whom the night brings counsel ; the *oncle à succession* and the pliant inheritor ; the little ninny who

insists that the *Moonlight Sonata* is by Mendelssohn.
I have a contempt for the Christian who looks down
upon the Jew, the white man who animadverts against
the black. I have a horror of the Freemason in his
cups ; of the players of solo-whist ; of the actor with
pretensions towards edification claiming to raddle his
face that ultimately fewer women may raddle theirs,
who 'asks a blessing' on his Hamlet. I hate the
commonplaces of the train, the street, and the market.
I abhor the belly of the successful man and the
swelling paunch of the Justice. But my particular
loathing is reserved for the unknowledgable fool who
says in his heart : " These things are not within my
experience ; therefore they cannot be true."

What a plague is *ennui* ! To have been everywhere,
seen everything, done everything, to have used up the
senses and let slip the supreme boon, is of all moral
diseases the last incurable. To be tired of oneself and
one's proficiencies, of the feel of a cue, the whip of a
club, the way the racquet comes up in the hand, the
touch of reins, the 'handle' of your favourite book,
all this is indeed to find the world flat and unpro-
fitable. Nothing remains, says your quack, but to
take his pills. Nothing remains but to follow my
system of exercises, declares some frock-coated
Hercules.

There is, we have often been told, valour and to
spare in the spirit's triumph over the flesh. But there
is ignominy, I take it, in a romantic spleen giving way
to massage, in a fine frenzy of melancholy yielding
before a system of exercises. I know nothing more
humiliating than this o'ercrowing of the spirit by the
body. Hamlet himself had done less girding at the
world if he had not been, as Gertrude remarks, in
poor condition. That the world is out of joint is an

old cry. It belongs to our day to advertise all that loss of figure and excess of flesh, baldness and superfluous hair, tuberculosis, which are our inheritance. I have never been able to fathom the delicate arts' survival of these natural shocks. Greatly in their favour has been the lateness of the world's discovery of electricity, X-rays, Swedish drills, and physical exercises. A Musset the picture of rude health, a Chopin who should dedicate a nocturne to Mr Sandow, a Shelley *père de famille*, a Baudelaire who should be an inside right to be reckoned with—these were unthinkable. But it is no part of the storyteller's business to argue, especially when he is not too sure of his case, and you could shatter mine by citing the admirable boxer who is responsible for *Pelléas and Mélisande*.

What I am driving at is that life is never as exquisite nor as tragic as it appears on the surface. I am plagued with a keen appreciation of the tendency of things to find their own level, and I see the world through common-sense spectacles. With me the exquisite moment is of short duration ; subsidence is always at hand. Grief is tragic, but its expression, except in the hands of the trained actor, grotesque. A woman in tears is the most monstrous of spectacles, birth as lamentable as death, the terror of many an honest execution marred by the vulgarity of the hangman and our vision of the glass which is to refresh him. What, we ask, remains for the fellow in the evening of his days save the decline to some barparlour ? Life is always taking the edge off things, and it is become the fashion to scoff at the monster and the grand *détraqué*. One laughs them out of existence, poor souls. Life is reasonable and sane ; your true realist will have nothing to do with *bravura*.

Life is exactly like a common-sensical novel by—never mind whom, and I fear sometimes lest the Ultimate Cause be made after that author's image. And yet the most modern writers have their cowardices. Which of them dares portray a murderer *bored* with the imbecile chunnerings, the senile irrelevancies of his judge? Which of them will attribute the clear eye and healthy appetite of the released convict less to the joy of freedom than to a *régime* of regular hours and enforced abstinences? They are afraid of their readers, and rightly. What reader would tolerate that I should set down my real feelings on nearing discharge? From me is expected relief from the intermittent panic, the perpetual dread, the nameless horror, whereas all I have to tell is of escape from an ecstasy of boredom. The truth is that even fear cannot endure for ever; the human mechanism has its limits. Soldiers have told of the power at the long last to put fear behind, not that desperate fear which is the moment of valour's catch in the throat, but the more serious dread, the dull foreboding of inaction. Man cannot keep his mind for ever on the rack; God is to be thanked that we have not complete control of our mentality. I have to reason myself to consciousness of the great deeds which are afoot; I have come to feel intuitively that death is cheapening and that it has become a little thing to die.

A little thing in one sense, how tremendous in another! My reverence for the common soldier exceeds all bounds. Even more vital than the compulsion to mete out to hellish torturers the measure they meted out to their helpless victims is the obligation of this country to see that no common soldier who has served in France shall ever know the meaning of want. It is for the nation to adopt its cripples and its maimed, to exact from the poor man his contribution of work and from the rich man even to one hundred per cent. of that which he hath, rather than that a single one of these unmurmuring brave should starve. Yesterday a man died in my ward, a man whom in ordinary times one would have dismissed as a drunkard and a lecherer. I am not content with these old classifications ; I am not content with a future life for this soldier which shall be all Michael Angelo and Sebastian Bach. There must be a paradise for the simpletons as for picked spirits. I am not content with a roll-call of the illustrious dead who shall arise to greet the coming of our latter-day heroes—great Edward and great Harry, the swingeing Elizabethan blade, businesslike Roundhead and inefficient Cavalier. Marlborough, Wellington, Napier, Nicholson, Havelock, Gordon— the shining list does not suffice. I am not content though Nelson return a millionfold the kiss he received from Hardy. I want a Valhalla which shall not be a palace, but a home. I think I could trust Lamb to make a sufficient welcome, though it is to Falstaff I should look to discourse of honour in a strain bearable to soldier ears. Nectar and ambrosia may be good taking, but there must be familiar grog and laughter and good-fellowship. I want a heaven in which horses shall be run, and the laying of odds allowed a sinless occupation. I want to see Sayers and Heenan fight it out again, to roar at Dan Leno, to watch old Grace till the shadows grow long.

The most bizarre conceptions assail me. I do not despair of finding a good terrier, a sufficiency of rats, and an unoccupied corner of the marble floor. I want not only the best the celestial architects may contrive in the way of saloons, but I want the atmosphere of bar-parlours ; I want pipes of clay and pint-pots of jasper, common briars and spittoons of jade. Out of doors, playing-fields with well-matched teams, keen-eyed umpires, hysterical supporters, and tapering goal-posts—chrysoprase if you insist, but common deal will do—and a feeling that once a week it will be Saturday afternoon.

I remember reading in some exquisite diary of the War this letter of a soldier :

DEAR MUM, AND DAD, AND LOVING SISTERS, ROSE, MABEL, AND OUR GLADYS,

I am very pleased to write you another welcome letter as this leaves me at present. Dear Mum and Dad and loving sisters, keep the home-fires burning. Not arf ! The boys are in the pink. Not arf ! Dear loving sisters, Rose, Mabel, and our Gladys, keep merry and bright. Not arf !

I place this amongst the most pathetic and most beautiful of the world's letters. It brings tears, and the refrain " Rose, Mabel, and our Gladys " has the plaintiveness of a litany.

I want a heaven for this writer that shall please him.

From "Responsibility"

ON HAVING FAVOURITES

ALLAN MONKHOUSE

THE other day a little girl told me that of all authors she considered Judge Parry to be the best, and I received some credit in being able to claim acquaintance with him. And I have a friend who places first among created beings (I don't think this is going too far) Madame Sarah Bernhardt. It is good that there should be such enthusiasms ; they bless him that gives and him that takes. That some one in the world should place you first, not because you are a husband or a lover or the head of something, but from sheer admiration and appreciation of what you've done, must be very heartening. Most of us, however, flatter ourselves that we are catholic, that we appreciate and admire in the right proportions, that we are above arbitrary prejudices. The sane critic may find it a little depressing to know how near he can come to agreement with another sane critic. And if you are a modest person arguing for this or for that it may come upon you that you are not quite so much in the right as you thought you were ; that you have become rigid in some old loyalty or that you have been led into some eccentricity. You must lop off the excrescence that you had fondly imagined to be individuality.

Yet it is difficult to steer accurately between conservatism and revolt. To the old fogey the handsomely bound classic carries an authority that becomes an obsession. These gorgeous or solid volumes have lain on Victorian tables in their thousands, and their contents have acquired a kind of sanctity. To the average reverential man of the passing generation it is incredible that the upstarts whose names are quoted so frequently and unnecessarily in the papers can be put on a level with the canonized ones. And then, perhaps, he may find himself reading something by Mr de la Mare and liking it better than what he had just read of Matthew Arnold's. So then he must read *The Scholar Gipsy* again to restore the balance, but in his heart he knows that these are not a god and a man, but two men. Arnold was the favourite poet of a friend of mine who died long ago. I don't think he was prepared to argue that Arnold was greater than Wordsworth or Keats ; only that he appealed more to him. And that is right. Let us have our favourites. We are not all exquisite critical machines, and it is bad to pretend to be. These poets have not an absolute stature, and we have, or should have, our idiosyncrasies, our queer individualities. I could believe that somewhere there is a quiet, obscure person whose favourite poet is Hood.

There is danger in getting your opinions pigeon-holed, certainly, and it may be unfair to those you have admired. A little book of essays recently published by Mr Hewlett has an introduction in which he complains that readers will pin down an author to their original conception of him. Thus, " it is still the fact that six readers out of ten expect every new book of mine that reaches them to be more or less of an echo of *The Forest Lovers*." And he can do nothing except foam at the mouth. *The Song of the Plow* is a greater work, but Mr Hewlett is an established favourite in the other line. Thomas Hardy, too, is always known as a novelist, though critics keep telling us that *The Dynasts* and the poems are more important (*I* don't believe it). By all means let us have our favourites, but don't let us treat them as subjects for petrifaction. Even the critic may find himself limited by what he has said or written. Far back in my own dark ages I wrote something about Gissing, and when I read it again many years later it seemed that I was exactly where I had been. If you write a thing down and have it printed it becomes an epitome to which you cling in a shifting world. Ask a reviewer what he thinks of a book, and he will repeat the heads of his review ; ask him years afterwards, and if he remembers anything at all he will give some hazy outline of that review. We are fixed, we are not open-minded enough, and yet perhaps it is worse to be too fluid. There is loyalty that is not mere rigidity, a loyalty to your sincere enthusiasms. I don't like people to tell me that Ruskin was a great man to them and that now he is nothing ; you cannot be right to throw people over like that ; the gods of your youth are not false gods.

I think that most reviewers are canny, moderate people who fear to make fools of themselves. They would like to discover and acclaim genius, but the pseudo-genius is a dangerous fellow. He has so often been taken at his own valuation ; the grandiose, the pretentious, with a bit of talent to help, may go a long way. Criticism wants both pluck and discretion, and I think sometimes that some of us might get on better if we could say simply what we like, and why, without bothering with formal criticism. It might be as well, though, before taking this course, to make ourselves as well-proportioned as we can. We strive

o

towards a just all-round appreciation, and it would
be disaster to attain it. The best fun is to have
favourites, but they must be real ones : they must
answer to something in our nature.

TIME, PLACE, AND BOOK

THOMAS BURKE

FOR the true lover of books there is a time and a place for the reading of each of his loved ones, when they give of their best. There is a sort of bookworm who will read any book anywhere at any time. I caught a man the other day reading Smollett in the Tube ; but that sort is no true lover. He does not taste his books ; he wolfs them, and, of course, misses the nuances of flavour and the essential grace which are yielded only in the suitable surroundings. And the suitable surroundings must be in contrast to the spirit of the book. Smollett and the Tube are too near to each other.

We do not, for example, on the cedared lawns of the country extract the best from what are called open-air books. They should be read in back rooms in crowded cities. I know that, for myself, the lines :

> Oh, it came o'er my ear like the sweet South
> That breathes upon a bank of violets
> Stealing and giving odour

effused far more of beauty when read in a bed-sitting-room in Kennington than when remembered in Surrey lanes.

I would never read Richard Jefferies on a hill-top. The reality kills the illusion. Books cannot live with leaves and skies and sunlight. The proper place for a Corot is on the walls of a room ; hanging from the bough of a tree it is an offence.

So with books about the town ; these best give their flavour in the quiet of a country cottage. Books of travel belong rightly to the fireside, not to the library of a liner. The authors most popular in the trenches were not the authors of books on physical adventure or exploration, or deeds that won the empire. The author most in demand among the non-literary was Nat Gould ; and among the literary, poets and quiet essayists.

Certain heretics will tell you that the term ' bedside book ' is a capricious classification, without basis in fact. I think they are wrong. I think there are decidedly books for the bedside, books for the library, books for the fireside, books for the tea-table, morning books, afternoon books, and evening books. A friend of mine even invented a magazine for the bathroom to be called the *H. and Cerial*.

Bed is assuredly the best place wherein to read tales of hairbreadth escapes and moving accidents. There you are cut off from the life presented to you, and even from the life of your own house or flat. If the telephone rings, let it ring. If the postman knocks, let him knock. You are undressed and in bed, three feet from the workaday floor, lifted above the world of planning and doing. You lie on clouds, god-like ; and are in the right mood to hear the tales of the stress and struggle of these mortals. Bed is the place for *Treasure Island* and *Kidnapped*. You can't get much out of Shackleton's *South* by reading it in a London bus on a foggy night ; you are preoccupied with a personal adventure of your own, and are therefore the less sensitive to it. Take it to bed with you. But don't take Swift, he is a thorny bed-fellow ;

and even Max Beerbohm and Anatole France are too shrewd to make good company.

For the winter fireside after dinner the boisterous picaresque novel is most agreeable—*Pickwick, Random, Gil Blas, Don Quixote*—or one of your gossips—Howell, of the *Familiar Letters*, Grammont, Pepys, Boswell, Evelyn, Captain Gronow.

Delicate or sophisticated writing suits the daytime. On the sunny morning or afternoon you may properly sit in the window with Jane Austen and Mrs Gaskell and Peacock, and *The Roadmender* and *The Compleat Angler*, and a good deal of Stevenson. Mrs Meynell's essays are for the afternoon ; *Lavengro*, or *The Bible in Spain*, are for the evening. I once attempted *The Imitation of Christ* in the evening, and had to lay it aside for Paterson's *Roads*, as in the summer I have had to drop Herman Melville and turn to *A Sentimental Journey*.

I have seen people reading—or pretending to read —on seaside parades and beaches. What sort of books, and whether they really read them, I don't know. I marvel at the mere attempt. In open sunlight I cannot take the sense of even a newspaper paragraph, and a page of a novel becomes a maze of words. A few of the elegant poets—Lovelace, Herrick, Campion, Daniel, Drummond, Drayton, Cowley—permit themselves to be read in the dusk of the summer-house or in a boat moored well under the trees ; but no printed page is entirely happy in the full glare of the sun.

Apart from bed, the best place I know for reading heroic stuff is an organ loft. During my last year at school I was organ-blower in the school chapel. There, during the sermon, address, and prayer, I was safe behind my green baize curtain. I was surrounded by an atmosphere of mystery and stained glass, and through a hole in one of the windows I could see hills and white roads, and hear the sound of horses.   Time and place were perfect for the purpose to which I put them—namely, the reading of Harrison Ainsworth.

FABLES AND FOLK-LORE

PAMELA GREY

BEFORE printing was invented, and before books were available, certain individuals were held high in the estimation of their fellow-men. They were the Story Tellers, people who had rich, ingenious minds ; or such as joined an excellent memory and a fine gift of expression to the invention of others. These may be looked on as among the benefactors of mankind, for their work is alive to-day. It is still helping and cheering mankind in the great store of fable and fairy-tale that belongs to every country. Their work will last as long as there are men and women to read and children to listen, because it is drawn from the very stuff of human nature itself. It has its living roots in a soil that is as fresh to-day as it was in the time of the earliest civilizations.

In one sense folk-lore is religious teaching. The word religion is one with the French word *relier*, comes from the Latin root *ligare* to bind, and if the word means ' to unite ' it is sufficiently pitiful to think how continually man has made religion to be a cause of severance. Now, folk-lore binds the greatest distances together, and unites us in showing us we are all kin. There is an Egyptian story that has the salient features of the story of Cinderella, which is of Scandinavian origin. Even such wide distances are spanned by the far reach of folk-lore's human touch.

America's *Rip-van-Winkle* is found in a Japanese story called *Urashima*, and there are many more such likenesses.

Now, what did this old habit of story-telling mean ? What were they about, these old people ? What were they doing with their fables and their tales ? The answer is, they were teaching all the time ; though they only set out to solace and amuse. And they would not have been half so successful if they had wanted to teach. It is just because they told of what they saw around them, the sorrows, the joys, the love, the craft, the courage, and the devotion, in short all the desperate grip of things that makes up the shining stuff of human nature, it is because they told us simply of all this that they hold before us so vividly a page of earthly existence. Let us look at a few of the myths and fairy-tales that we have all listened to as children. They hold great lessons : telling, for instance, of the beauty of compassion over callousness. When we read of the fairy godmother's power overcoming the cruel stepmother, doesn't the beauty of kindness shine plainly here ? And when we read of the prince who had always such difficulties to overcome, who was told he must never look back but always go straight on, and succeed by constant endeavour. We didn't know as we read that we were understanding what a good thing it is to endure. Then think of the manner in which these lovely old stories always taught that nothing good was ever wasted. Not the smallest good action but had its inevitable result. How safely the tale went on, with all the children listening, and something within them saying, " That is what does happen, only sometimes one doesn't see the end of things here." Think for a moment, too, of the princesses that were shut up in dark towers, guarded by the most frightful dragons ; but no power in the world could prevent, in the end, something quite wonderfully delightful happening to them if they were good. The steepest walls were scaled and the mountain of glass was put behind them, all to show how material things are quite malleable if we know how to deal with them, and that there is something much stronger than dragons—which symbolize evil. In short, " stone walls do not a prison make, nor iron bars a cage," for the power of mind may convert such things " into an hermitage."

And this wisdom is taught in all countries. It belongs to the human race, however little use it is put to.

Here is a Japanese story about a robber and a spider. An unusual juxtaposition indeed ; but the moral of the story will need no explanation. It is beautifully lucid and simple, and it is ages old. It tells that in Japan long ago there was a famous robber. He was known for his wicked deeds and evil life, and in the course of time when he was killed, he found himself far down in the infernal regions. Many years he dwelt there till the time came when the Light of the East, the Lord Buddha, was to visit those realms of uttermost darkness ; for there is no region so dark but that the ray of his light, from time to time, penetrates its gloom. Turning to him the robber exclaimed, " Oh, let me raise myself from this dark abode, let me return to a lighter region ! " And the Lord Buddha, he who is the Blameless One, the Awakened, said to him, " Can you remember any kind deed you did on earth that might help you now ? " Then the robber set about turning memories over in his miserable mind, looking for some good action. " Yes," he answered ; " once

when I was walking through a wood there was a
spider in my path and I might have set my foot upon
it, but I lifted it out of the way for it was enjoying
the sunshine." And the Awakened One smiled and
went on his way of mercy. Then the robber saw in
the darkness a tiny silken thread. It hung down
before him and he recognized it as the spider's web,
with light upon it. Eagerly he stretched out his
hands and clasped it, and to his wonder he found
that it could bear his weight. Quickly he slung himself up, leaving his miserable condition behind him.
And soon he saw the light of the sun and felt the
warm air touching him. But as he was still climbing
he became aware of a great murmur behind him,
and looking back over his shoulder he saw all the
denizens of the dark abode climbing up his spider-
web after him. And the spider's web bore them all.
Hundreds and hundreds of them were climbing towards the light, and the murmur of the great multitude was growing ever louder and louder. Then the
robber was filled with a great fear lest the spider-web
could not support them, and he thought only of his
own safety. " Get back," he cried, " get back all of
you ! It's mine ! " And just as he said the words
the spider-web broke, and he fell down, down, down
to the gloom from whence he had arisen. We can
readily see what this story teaches ; there is no need
to hammer the shining metal thin.

Take this other Eastern story, just as humorous as
the other is serious. It is called the story of *The
Fakir and the Cooking-pot*. It teaches that those who
want to get the better of their fellows in any dishonest
way may very neatly get hit by their own stick.
There was once an old fakir, one who lives in prayer
and poverty, subsisting on the food given to him by

others in recognition of his virtue. One day this old
fakir appeared at the door of his neighbour's house
and said : " Can you give me the loan of a cooking-
pot to make something savoury of that which a kind
brother has given me ? " The neighbour lent him a
cooking-pot, and he went away with it to his cave.
After a few days the neighbour expected him to return it, but as he never arrived the neighbour went
to the fakir to claim his own. When he got there a
surprise was in store for him. " Give you back your
cooking-pot," the old fakir said, " I would in a
moment if I could, but I can't just now, and I will
tell you the reason. The truth is, a very wonderful
thing has happened. Your cooking-pot has had a
young one ! I wouldn't disturb it for the world."
" Well," the neighbour thought, " this is a crazy old
man " ; but he said : " What do you mean ? How
can a cooking-pot have a young one ? " " You just
come and see," said the old fakir, and he went into
his cave and pointed to a rough shelf in the rock ;
and there, sure enough, the neighbour saw his own
cooking-pot, with a little cooking-pot close beside it.
" Ah-ha ! " he thought, " this is very good. Of
course the old man is crazy, but it is all the better
for me, because I shall get two cooking-pots back
when the time comes for returning." And aloud he
said : " I see ! You are perfectly right ! I will
come again for them in a fortnight." At the end
of that time he appeared once more at the fakir's
cave. " I've come for the cooking-pots," he said.
" Oh, I have very sad news for you," the old fakir
answered. " Your cooking-pot is dead. Yes, it died ;
in fact they both died ; soon after you left. It is
the regretful truth, but I mustn't hold it from you."
Then the neighbour was very angry. " Dead ! " he

exclaimed. " The cooking-pot dead ! Who in a long
life heard of a cooking-pot dying ? Give me back
my property at once, I've had enough of your tales."
" Ah," said the other, " you believed me when I told
you the cooking-pot had had a young one, because
it was in your interest to do so ; and you will have
to believe me now, when I tell you it has died, because this is not a bit more improbable." So the
neighbour had to go home and realize that the fakir
had caught him adroitly. But isn't the humour of
the thing heightened by its being a ' holy man ' who
was so very nimble in doubling his earthly goods ?

Foremost in the literature of folk-lore stand the Border Ballads. What a moving page ! Love and passion,
slander and censure, courage and infamy, blessing
and cursing, in short, deeds done ill or well, the
narrative throbs and pulses as the human lot is told.
And, mind you, there is no author's name to the
verses. The anonymity of the Border Ballads is one
of the astounding facts in literature. Perhaps it is
because they are so universal that they cannot be
ascribed to any one name. Let us look at the ballad
that is named *Fair Flowers in the Valley*. It tells of
the sorrowfullest happening that can follow per-
fidious love, when a lonely mother takes the life of
her infant, the very sight of which is more than she
can bear. It is an old story, and the strength of it
lies in this, that with an inimitable touch the beauty
of Nature is repeatedly alluded to, in a recurring
refrain, giving the force of contrast. The sheer art
achieved in the design of the thing is consummate,
and it is as simple as a sigh. First, you have the
event put baldly before you. You are told of the
tragic deed that follows, you hear the judgment
sounding at the close in the recognition of guilt and

the realization of the suffering that must follow; and all the time, like a soft wind blowing through summer branches, close up against this tragedy you have the quiet words : " And the green leaves they grow rarely."

She laid her down beneath the thorn,
 Fair flowers in the valley,
And there she had her sweet babe born.
 And the green leaves they grow rarely.

" Smile na sae sweet, my bonnie babe ! "
 Fair flowers in the valley,
" Smile na sae sweet, gin ye smile me deid ! "
 And the green leaves they grow rarely.

She has ta'en out her littel knife,
 Fair flowers in the valley,
And twined the sweet babe of its life.
 And the green leaves they grow rarely.

As she was coming frae the Church,
 Fair flowers in the valley,
She sees a small babe in the porch.
 And the green leaves they grow rarely.

" Oh, bonny babe ! gin ye were mine,"
 Fair flowers in the valley,
" I would clad you in silk and sabelline ! "
 And the green leaves they grow rarely.

" When I was thine, O Mother mine,"
 Fair flowers in the valley,
" Ye were not then sae sweet and kind."
 And the green leaves they grow rarely.

" But now I sleep on Mary's knee,"
 Fair flowers in the valley,
" And ye have the pains of Hell to dree."
 And the green leaves they grow rarely.

Mankind does much to spoil this lovely earth, and the green leaves still grow rarely, and however sinful and sorrowful we may be there are still fair flowers in the valley. You would think that we must blacken

things, but it is not so ; and the manner in which
the ballad brings out this point so simply is what
makes it the immortal verse it is. The constancy
of Nature, and its imperishable beauty. Another
way of saying " Underneath are the Everlasting
Arms."

Then there is the great ballad called *The Wife of
Usher's Well*. This has for its theme a matter of
passing interest. It deals with the love that is stronger
than death, that penetrates the veil of death. The
love that brings the souls of those, so often and so
wrongly called the ' departed,' once again into the
earthly vision of the bereaved, so that the mourner
is convinced of their continued existence, and is
comforted. The great point to be noticed here is
that when the mother sees the spirits of her dead
sons, she sees them dressed in their earthly garments.
They are wearing the clothes she recognizes, and yet,
in one line—a master-stroke—we are told that these
clothes were not of earthly origin. Yet they are
dressed as she remembers them, they are ' happed '
around with her mantle. She lays them to rest upon
her bed. The point to be taken is that they are
actually there with her ; and they are there because
of the greatness of her longing that they should be
so. The force of this old ballad, its simplicity of
narrative and event, remind you as you read of some
of the stories in the New Testament.

> There lived a wife at Usher's Well,
>   And a wealthy wife was she ;
> She had three stout and stalwart sons,
>   And sent them o'er the sea.
>
> They hadna been a week from her,
>   A week but barely ane,
> When word cam' to the carline wife
>   That her three sons were gane.

They hadna been a week from her,
  A week but barely three,
When word cam' to the carline wife
  That her sons she'd never see.

" I wish the wind may never cease,
  Nor fashes in the flood,
Till my three sons come hame to me
  In earthly flesh and blood."

It fell about the Martinmas,
  When nights are lang and mirk,
The carline wife's three sons cam' home,
  And their hats were o' the birk.

It never grew in syke nor ditch,
  Nor yet in ony sheugh ;
But at the gates o' Paradise
  That birk grew fair eneugh.

" Blow up the fire now, maidens mine,
  Bring water from the well !
For all my house shall feast this night,
  Since my three sons are well."

And she has made to them a bed,
  She's made it large and wide ;
And she's ta'en her mantle her about,
  Sat down at the bedside.

Up then crew the red, red cock,
  And up and crew the grey ;
The eldest to the youngest said,
  " 'Tis time we were away."

" The cock doth craw, the day doth daw',
  The channerin' worm doth chide ;
Gin we are missed out o' our place,
  A sair pain we maun bide."

" Lie still, lie still but a little wee while,
  Lie still but if we may ;
Gin my mother should miss us when she wakes
  She'll go mad e'er it be day."

O they've ta'en up their mother's mantle,
  And they've hung it on a pin.
" O lang may ye hing, my mother's mantle,
  Ere ye hap us again !

" Fare ye weel, my mother dear !
    Fareweel to barn and byre !
And fare ye weel, the bonny lass
    That kindles my mother's fire."

You may find among the ballads variants of the
same theme, just as you may find variants of the
same fairy-story in different countries, and it is
interesting to follow some of these. One idea that
often occurs is the mercy shown by God to erring
mortals. In one form we are told of a nun who
spent years of prayer and self-sacrifice in a convent,
but who was tormented ceaselessly by a great longing
to escape. One night she is given the duty of guarding the convent door, and during the long hours
temptation comes strongly upon her to join in the
outer life. She sees through the grating the open
country, and the lights of the town in the valley,
where a festival is being held. The desire to break
her bonds overmasters her, and she leaves her post,
deserting her duty and breaking her vows. All night
she revels with the crowd joining in the carnival, and
late in the grey dawn, utterly broken and sorrowful,
she steals back to the convent on the hill.

And when she comes to the grated door thinking
she will be denounced by her Superior, and degraded
for ever, she hears the bolts drawn back and she sees
a veiled form standing there in the likeness of herself,
with a great light shining around. Then it becomes
clear to her that the Virgin Mary herself has taken
her place, and kept the door for her all night so that
her fault should not be discovered ; and this because
her better self had never consented to her sin. You
find this central idea in other forms. It tells of a
high spirit ministering on earth when human nature,
through weakness or weariness, cannot support the
load.

" Now let us praise famous men, and our fathers that begat us. . . . Such as found out musical tunes, and such as recited verses in writing. . . ." For they have left us a great heritage. Their words in song and story are with us still. Just as we may look into clear water and see an image of the moon, so we can look upon the pages of Folk-lore and see there mirrored an image of the Spirit of Man ; a thing not without blemishes, but holding nevertheless a something without which our night would be dark indeed. It is this which lights Man's long pilgrimage. Like the Moon it gives the reflection of a light far greater than itself, something far brighter, far loftier, than anything we can directly gaze upon ; but it bears testimony to a light which we know is there, and which shines for all.

From " Shepherd's Crowns "

P

CINDERELLA

ROBERT BLATCHFORD

THERE are two wicker armchairs in the hall of the Hôtel Vert : one each side the entrance to the ladies' boudoir. They are conspicuous and large chairs with widespread and inviting arms, and are placed almost immediately under the arc light. It was in these chairs the sisters sat : two English women, dressed in black.

The plain sister took the chair on the left and the pretty sister the chair on the right of the door. The pretty sister was not pretty, really ; she was one of those women who habitually look more than their best. The plain sister was frankly and unmistakably plain.

It was the contrast between these sisters, a contrast accentuated by their strong likeness to each other, which attracted my attention and held it.

The plain sister was certainly ten years senior to the pretty one ; the pretty one would be twenty-eight. The younger had a husband, a grave, ungainly man, with pale blue eyes, and pale yellow hair, worn thin on the top. The elder was a spinster.

The pretty sister was in all visible essentials an improved copy of the plain one. She was a little taller, and a little plumper, with better shoulders, and a trimmer waist. Her black dress fitted her more perfectly ; her hands were whiter ; her complexion was fairer ; she had more colour ; her hair was darker,

226

more plentiful, less neutral, of a chestnut shade. She had neat feet and neater shoes. She had two gold bangles ; her sister none. She had a silver belt ; her sister had a velvet band. She had two red roses at her breast ; her sister never a flower.

The pretty sister was the gayer, though both were vivacious ; she had a quicker, brighter, darker eye. When she smiled she turned her full lips up at the corners, while her sister turned her thin lips down.

The plain sister was reading Baedeker ; the pretty one had a volume of Swinburne, from which she seemed to read passages now and again to her companion. There must have been quite two yards of space between their chairs, yet her sister seemed to hear what she was reading. When the quotations stopped the plain sister returned to Baedeker and the light died out of her eyes.

Presently the husband joined the ladies. He sat beside the pretty one, to whom he addressed most of his remarks. Both the ladies seemed amused by his conversation ; but the plain one only smiled, whereas the pretty one often laughed. Presently a waiter was called. The husband then spoke to the pretty sister, who evidently translated the order. I noticed that it was always she who addressed the servants or officials of the hotel ; the plain sister had no French. When the order was executed the plain sister took coffee ; the pretty one took wine.

When the party retired the wife spoke to the lift attendant, the spinster collected the wraps and other feminine impedimenta. As they were about entering the lift another English couple came in and crossed the hall to speak to them. As I expected, the pretty sister gave them a bright and animated greeting, while the plain one provided her usual paler copy.

The newcomers talked for a little, almost wholly to the pretty wife, who sparkled and rippled in her voluble replies. Then they parted, and the sisters went aloft, while the husband strolled away to finish his cigar.

That is all my story. One might sit during such a little scene and conjure up romance and comedy out of the performance, but it seems that no vagary of the imagination is required in such a case. Here were two women, daughters of the same mother. One had prettiness, gaiety, and charm ; the other was her foil, her unsuccessful echo. One had youth, talent, riches, a husband, troops of friends. The other was a spinster and a mere appendage to her triumph. What had the elder sister done to offend the gods ? Why had Fortune dropped all the coins and *bonbons* in the younger's shoe ?

If the elder sister had got the luck, would she have been still the plain one ? If she had been the prettier sister, would her charms have brought the luck ? Unto her that hath much shall more be given ; but why ? Surely Nature or the gods had been unfair. For if this were a matter of deserving one could not help but feel that the spoils had fallen as in life they so often do fall, to the more insistent and pre-datory spear.

One needed not two glances to discover that the prettier woman possessed more of what the economists call effective demand. It was the elder who would the sooner give way ; it was the younger whose desire had the keener edge, whose hand more readily as well as more gracefully took the sweetest flower or the ripest peach. Husband, sister, friends, the world, and Fate conspired to make the easier way luxurious. Because she was the better armed, the fuller gifted, and more richly endowed of the two, all her circle acquiesced in the payment of the tribute she exacted. They strewed their blossoms in her path, they painted her lilies, and refined her gold ; they brought her butter in a lordly dish.

This is an old trick of the world ; it is an old twist in Fortune's favour against which the just, the pitiful, and the idealist have for centuries of centuries striven in vain. It is the old injustice of Heaven which Science has named " survival of the fittest."

What child reader of *Cinderella* has ever felt a pang for the ugly sisters ? They were envious and harsh, those less favoured women ; but, perhaps, to be ill-favoured does not conduce to amiability and magnanimity. And Miss Cinderella, with her little feet and her pretty face, did she merit all the opulence of love and riches heaped upon her ? To be young ; to be beautiful ; to be charming ; to be good ; and, withal, to have small feet—are not these enough of blessings that to them must be added the prizes of a princely husband, a life of happiness ever after, and an immortality of juvenile sympathy and admiration ?

What did the ugly sisters think ? How could an ugly sister, with a chronic pain in her temper and big feet, be expected to fight against Fate, Nature, and a fairy godmother ?

As I sat with my pipe and my coffee after those two sisters had gone to bed in the Hôtel Vert I began to ask myself these questions, and I resolved to speak for the ugly sisters just one word.

After all, how do we know that the history of Cinderella has not been garbled ? If the historian or reporter of the period were personally acquainted with the ladies we may guess on whose side he would be. Cinderella, the pretty minx, who would know how to bedevil a mere male person. Since the gods had given her beauty (and small feet), and a fairy godmother had given her a coach and horses and a dress that was a dream, and since the prince had given her his love and his hand, it is asking too much of human nature to ask the special reporter of the *Daily Calythumpian* of the period for justice.

Who will be just to the ugly, to the ineffectual, to the defeated ; as against the beautiful, the successful, and the strong ?

The two ladies I saw in the Hôtel Vert would have made an excellent subject for the subtle and delicate art of Henry James ; but now that Thackeray is dead who shall write us the story of the Glass Slipper as told by Cinderella's elderly, ugly sister ?

THE HISTORY OF THE CLOTHES WE WEAR

DION CLAYTON CALTHROP

VERY few gentlemen walking the streets have the least idea that they carry on their backs a crabbed catalogue of English History, that they are sandwichmen advertising the past ages. Ladies who fly yearly into the past, ransack the world from top to toe for new ideas, and vary their figures to suit the fashion, know also just as little of the interesting thing they are doing. From the Egyptian hobble skirt to the trousers of the Turk is a far cry.

Men, however, can date the day on which the true modern clothes began for them and, with a little knowledge, can see how they have sunk to the present prevailing ugliness from the fair and fine creatures they were. Bag-wigs, gentlemen, swords and ruffles, full-skirted coats of peach-coloured silk, diamond buckles and roses " worth a family," where are they now ? We look like so many clerks hesitating between mourning and vulgarity.

On the thirteenth of October, 1666, King Charles the Second, having read John Evelyn's pamphlet entitled *Tyrannus, or the Mode*, became enamoured of the idea of the Persian coat. He had one made. So had the Duke of York. They tried them on.

Picture to yourself the fifteenth of October, when they first wore them in public. A far more drastic change than the changes of to-day, a far more amazing sight than the first harem trousers, or the close-fitting dress of the Directoire, for they were an utter and complete renunciation of all tradition. It is the violent change from the tunic of the Middle Ages to the ancestor of the frock-coat of to-day. Mr Pepys describes it : " A long cassocke close to the body of black cloth, and pinked with white silk under it, and a coat over it, the legs ruffled with black ribband like a pigeon's legs."

There's a point there, take heed of it. In other words, this was a black frock-coat, the first black frock-coat. Would that it had been the last !

On October the seventeenth the King saw Lord St Albans in an all-black suit, and, discarding his own black and white, which he said made him look too like a magpie, he ordered one all of black velvet. Sir Philip Howard, if you please, an extremist in the new Eastern fashion, wore a nightgown and turban like a Turk.

On November the twenty-second of the same year King Louis the Fourteenth of France, having a quarrel with King Charles, said that he would dress all his footmen in vests like the King of England. But the new fashion conquered in the end, and all the fashionable world with one accord gave up the little short tunic and the petticoat-breeches, and the infinity of ribbands, and went into frock-coats.

From thence to our own day the frock-coat has been the base of all our sartorial efforts. The cuffs altered, grew small, grew huge, narrowed, were split, and finally gave us the cuff of to-day. Our cuffs still carry the marks of their birth in the now useless row of buttons that adorn them. The costermonger alone has kept faithful to the turned-back real cuff, which, though we use it occasionally, is nearly dead.

The costermonger is one of the most interesting and complete survivals of an earlier age, for his coat with its square skirts, deep-flapped pockets, velvet and button ornaments, and his long waistcoat, likewise ornamented, is pure Georgian, while his striped jersey and bell-bottomed trousers are the very cut of the old sailor ; the trousers, as they say down East, " cut saucy over the trotters." Like every other historic part of our raiment, the cuff has shrunk into nothingness, and in the present day its width is measured only by the few inches necessary to allow of the appearance of the shirt-cuffs.

In 1727 we find the world getting a little more modern, frock-coat, waistcoat, and tie, but still there is the cocked hat and the wig. It is the wig that really divides us sharply from the past, those wonderful erections, staircase-wigs, cut-bobs, long-bobs, pigeon-wings, clubs, cornets, grizzle-majors, and all the host of bag-wigs, the remains of which are only to be seen in judges, barristers, coachmen, and in the powdered hair of menservants. The bag of the wigs remains on the tunics of the Welsh Fusiliers, on the coat-collars of certain coachmen, and on the Court suit. One other very curious thing remains in connexion with the cocked hat and wig, and that is the *aiguillettes*, or shoulder-knots, on the left shoulder of *aides-de-camp* and footmen. Mr Caton Woodville suggests that these long gold cords that pass under the shoulder as well as before, and are looped on to the top button of the tunic, are the cords of the cocked hat of the Marlburian soldier.

The *aides-de-camp* were then mounted on light, fast horses, and in order to guard the very expensive full-bottomed wig and heavy hat, they passed the long cords of their hats through the wig, round the shoulder, and looped them on the top button of their coats. This is a very likely suggestion, though it has also been said that they are a portion of the old bandolier, the remains of which are to be found in the chains and prickers of the Hussars' shoulder-belt.

From the Georgian full-skirted coat we get the two buttons that remain on the back of our frock- and tail-coats, where they were once placed to hold back the skirts while riding ; and we get also the footman's vertical pockets with buttoned flaps, which were once slits through which the sword-hilt passed.

The first black necktie was the Steinkirk, worn during the wars in Flanders and twisted instead of being elaborately folded, as the soldiers had no time for dandyism. Ties indeed are of the most ancient origin, and there are volumes of Cravatiana. The first ties are probably those worn by Roman orators to protect their throats—the *focalia* or orator's chin-cloth. Both Napoleon and Beau Brummell were very particular about their cravats, and both, curiously enough, changed them for the first time in their lives on the morning of their great defeats. Napoleon, who always wore a black silk tie, appeared on the morning of Waterloo with a flowing tie of white ; and Brummell, who always wore a white linen tie round a twelve-inch folded collar, wore a black silk tie just before he died in poverty at Caen.

Great men have often been particular about their clothes. Brummell invented the modern dress-suit and the first black dress-trousers and white evening waistcoat. Napoleon's grey coat marks him well in our eyes, and, besides that, he had a perfect passion for clothes, and arranged and overlooked all the suits and dresses for his coronation. Byron is known by his open loose collars in the days of the stiff-starched neckcloth. The Iron Duke is said to have sat for hours regarding himself before a glass in his peer's robes. George the Fourth, who, if he was not great, was at least notorious, invented a shoe-buckle. And almost the last person whom one would accuse of dandyism, George Washington, wrote a minute and complete order for his coats to his tailors, from a Newmarket coat with a hood, down to a dress-coat, for every buttonhole of which he sent the measurements.

As for Brummell, he alone is responsible for the English idea of cleanliness in clothes. He it was who had his neckcloths slightly starched to counteract the slovenly, sloppy ties of his day. He it was who really invented the constant use of clean linen, the appearance of what we call 'smartness,' the regular uniform dress of a gentleman both for morning and evening. His blue cloth coat with brass buttons shaped like our present evening-dress coats, except that they buttoned across ; his buff-coloured waistcoat with the slip of a thinner waistcoat showing above the buff ; his boots, of which he was proud to the last days before he went mad, varnished with *vernis de Guiton* ; his primrose-coloured gloves and top-hat and cane were to the fashionable world of his day the last word in dress. He is responsible for our uniform appearance in the evening ; and one may imagine him folding his collar and tying his tie, the first of our kind, whose ghost looks over our shoulders and shudders at our awkward attempts.

Why don't we wear blue coats for evening-dress now ? Our dress-clothes are really very dull, even the waistcoat-buttons are quiet and subdued. White is undoubtedly the colour for the shirt, the tie, and the waistcoat, and black for the trousers, but a blue coat would be a real relief : witness the effect of hunting-pink at a dance.

If it were not for women, the streets and restaurants, the parks and promenades would look for all the world like the remnants of a cheap funeral, as if the nation had never been able to get over the death of Dickens. Even the white top-hat has recently almost vanished, and colours seem to remain only in the vivid socks of undergraduates, and the wonderful waistcoats of the sportsmen. Racing, of all the sports, has kept up its tradition of the wearing of odd clothes. Since the days of George the First, when sporting men pushed back their wigs to show the natural colour of their hair underneath, the sporting man has pushed back whatever he wore on his head, and the angle of the billycock proclaims the man—the billycock being the hat once made for William Coke, of Norfolk, by Mr Bowler, the hatter, of Houndsditch : Billy Coke's hat.

When the riding-chairs called cabriolets came in from France in 1751, it was not only the sporting, but the most fashionable thing to ride in them, and not only to ride in them, but to wear patches on the face to represent them, and to have them embroidered on waistcoats, and to have the hair dressed like them in form. And the cab, later improved by Mr Hansom, became an emblem of the sporting idea in England. It provoked a new dress just as the motor-car has done. It gave us the Gentleman Joe coat with huge pearl buttons, and the curly-brimmed top-hat, and the thick dogskin driving-gloves, all of which, with very tight trousers, were worn by young gentlemen utterly innocent of cab-driving, and by them paraded in the streets with a sprig of geranium in the buttonhole, a straw in the mouth, and a reckless hat of curly brim or of nearly no brim at all. And it was all very gay and splendid. Now gentlemen equally innocent of motor-car knowledge wear leather-lined coats of voluminous size, and affect an anxious, nervous appearance and an absent manner. How gorgeously young the world is !

History, straying from the dressing-room, lingers in the hall. The very marks on the backs of our gloves come to us from the time when the fingers were embroidered. Look at the three middle fingers of your hand and you will see exactly how, by carrying down the embroidery between the fingers, the three points on our gloves are arrived at. And there they remain. Why these things remain that have long ceased to have rhyme or reason is a mystery, and can only be explained by remembering how long, how very long, it takes to kill anything in such a conservative country as ours, or indeed in any country, for I think that all men are at heart Conservatives.

We keep about our dress so many odd, needless, quaint things that it is almost a wonder we don't keep more, despite the tendency of the age that seeks to level everything into a series of grey numbered slabs. By rights we should all be dressed like seals in a smooth black waterproof covering, but thank goodness even the Upper Norwood Cricket Club cannot exist without colours, and blazers burst forth from myriad clubs every summer, and Margate Pier looks like a mad dream of heraldry.

With the gloves in the hall is a silk hat. Concerning this very type of hat, I find the following delightful story in Mr Clinch's book on costume. The first silk hat ever worn in London was worn by John Hetherington, a haberdasher of the Strand, on January 15th, 1797. He appeared on the street, and at once a great crowd collected, so great that several women fainted, and children screamed and dogs barked, and a young son of Cordwainer Thomas, who was returning from a chandler's shop, was thrown down and had his arm broken. Mr Hetherington was arraigned before the Lord Mayor on a charge of breach of the peace and inciting to riot, and was required to give bonds in the sum of £500. The evidence went to show that Mr Hetherington appeared on the highway wearing upon his head what he called a silk hat, a tall structure having a shiny lustre, and calculated to frighten timid people. Mr Clinch, quoting from one of the London papers of the time, says : " The new hat is destined to work a revolution in headgear, and we think the officers of the Crown erred in placing the defendant under arrest."

This goes to show that the harem skirt is not the first garment to raise a riot. The silk hat did not come from the East, although the shape has some fellowship with the hat of the Greek priest, but so many of our garments are derived from the East that one wonders at the outcry at the Turkish trousers. Certainly in the reign of Richard the First our streets and roads presented quite an Oriental appearance, for men swathed themselves in draperies and women wore stuffs from Eastern looms, and many were the Eastern customs brought home from the wars in the Holy Land.

So many things remain in our clothes of the past ages that, once we begin to analyse, we seem to put on the whole History of Man after our morning bath. Our socks—good heavens, our socks !—take us miles away from home, so that we lose ourselves in vague unknown dates. Our pumps are absolutely Eliza-

bethan. " Get good strings to your beards, new
ribbons to your pumps," says Shakespeare. Our
shirts ! Look along history's washing-list and see
how we have come from the plain shirt-vest with a
button and loop, such as the Egyptians wore, to
Tudor shirts with collars and cuffs and fronts embroidered with black silk, and shirts to hold huge
ruffs like cartwheels, and, behold, the ruffs fall flat,
unstarched, and become Vandyke collars, and these
become the Puritan bands still worn by barristers
and bishops, and be-ribboned shirts home from the
wars in Flanders, and shirts for Dr Johnson to dirty
with snuff and tea-stains, and shirts washed at Wey-
mouth while Farmer George enters the water to the
strains of a band, and shirts with the studied neglect
of Byron and the precise and exquisite propriety of
Brummell, till we reach our own hideous conven-
tional garment of boiled rag armour with its stiff
cuffs.

Then to our brogue shoes, all fitted with ornament
like a Roman sandal, just in the selfsame way. Then
trousers, monuments of antiquity far beyond the pale
of mere guesses, the most ancient of garments, and
showing in their shape but one peculiar survival, and
that in the silk braid down the outside seams of
dress-trousers. These are the survivals of the times
when the tight military trousers unbuttoned down
the side to allow of the wearing of top-boots underneath, and the buttons were covered by a flap lined
sometimes with a colour. It is this flap that remains,
and it is by reason of this that military trousers boast
the broad red band.

In all this, in the putting on of all these garments,
you may notice one very peculiar and interesting fact,
that whereas a man always without exception has his

buttons on the right side of his clothes, a woman always has them on the left. It has been suggested that this peculiarity arises from the habit of women carrying children mostly on the left arm, and that it would be more convenient to carry the buttonhole on the right side over to the button on the left, and so, in closing the garment worn over the breast, not to disturb the child asleep. Also, that the man, in order to keep his right arm free, should carry the buttonhole over from the left to the button on the right. This discussion would seem finicking were it not for the insistence of a peculiarity that must have had at some time a very definite and necessary reason.

Buttons, of course, are a history in themselves. The boy Buttons, the successor to the Tiger, who was a very small boy who rode behind every smart turn-out, wears a perfect feast of buttons arranged like a skeleton suit such as Jackanapes wore. And a careful study of club servants reveals the most curious dispositions of buttons, all bound by strict laws of below-stairs, and showing that the higher a man rises in his profession as a servant the fewer buttons he wears. The boy in the hall wears the most, the hall-porter has so many on his cuffs, pockets, and the tail of his coat, the house-servants in their order wear an exact number of buttons, right up to the house-steward, who wears just as many buttons as a gentleman, and looks like a guest except that he has more dignity. In like manner do the maids as they go up discard the cap and white apron for the lace cap and black silk apron of the housekeeper. Aprons, indeed, occupy a large part of the world's wardrobe : green baize ; the white of the grocer ; the blue and white of the butcher ; the black of the bishop.

The three most interesting survivals actually in our

streets are the clothes of the Bluecoat boy, the black jacket of the Eton boy, and the cockade in coach-men's hats.

The Bluecoat boy is familiar enough in his long gown of Edward the Sixth's time, his black knee-breeches and yellow stockings and buckled shoes that are all Georgian, and his bands that are Geneva bands. The Eton boy's black suit and tall hat were first worn in black in mourning for George the Third. The cockade is the remains of the old chaperon, or hood, worn in the colours of their masters by the menservants all through the fourteenth century, and remaining now complete in shape, with that cut edge of the hood sticking out fan-shape and the curl of the liripipe twisted round in a neat coil. This hood remains also on the shoulder of the Garter mantle and in the dress of the French barrister.

Every year these interesting survivals become more rare ; one feels that the butcher will discard his apron, the confectioner his white cap, the cook his double-breasted white jacket, the last growler-driver his last cape. The Georgian dustman with his knee-breeches and white stockings has not long gone ; the Bluecoat boy has not long discarded his Statute Cap ; the Scotsman will lose his Glengarry with the strings, and the powdered flunkey is a dying race. So much to-day is utilitarian, and we do not indulge in enough foolishness ; and the protection of ancient remains of clothes is a good thing, for it serves to remind a forgetful generation of the history of its country.

The splendid comedy of the streets still goes on, lightened here and there by a dandy, by the red flare of a Guardsman's big coat, by a much befurred motorist, by the uniform of bank messengers and the importance of commissionaires. Our bus-driver

Q

swaddled against the cold has nearly gone, gone to give place to grimy, dull mechanics, whose attire is a negative of all the arts of dress. Our fine cab-drivers with their suggestion of decayed aristocracy have given way before a race of uniformed officials with apparently uniform minds. But women are the flowers of the pavements, a constantly changing stream of shapes and colours ; they know no stern account of history, and change so quickly from bishop sleeves to Empire gowns, and from Empire figures to hobbled sausage-like bodies, that mere man cannot tell what his wife will look like next month. This is why woman has no place in the search for the origin of things ; her charm is eternal, nothing withers her infinite variety, nothing disturbs her ever-changing mood. The brilliant colours of the silks set out to catch her eye make our gay streets sing with colour harmonies. Her secrets now are set in all the shops, her figure mocks us from the corset-maker's window, her hair is all displayed in the full light of the hairdresser's establishments ; all the openwork *lingerie*, cases for her dainty feet, polish for her dainty nails, rouge for her fading cheeks are unblushingly set out before us, yet for all this knowledge, even as when in toyshops the conjurer's tricks are given away, we cannot piece her together as a living, breathing, historical creature as we can a man, for when we set up our dummy to write a little essay on her kind no life is there. We are as steady as rocks, wearing all the tags and bobtails of older civilizations, keeping our old customs and costumes so that we may see ourselves the mirrors of other days, but she, elusive ever, the living embroidery of life, discards a century or so every season, wears Directoire clothes for a second, and when we seek to pin her down, behold, she walks like a king's daughter in Turkish trousers, or floats before us in a cloud of silks, or catches the tropics in one hand and wears them in her hat.

For all this women may and do laugh at us. We do change our figures, but so quietly that not one notices it until they look back along the tailors' books and see us only eighty years ago, or even fifty years ago, and but a step less, the day before automobilism, when we knew not black leather coats, or goggles, or German-looking caps, and were still on the horsey side for choice and very particular to wear frock-coats and top-hats in Piccadilly and observe all the correctness of Bond Street. Petrol is helping to kill dandies, alas ; and I am all for a nation of well-dressed people, as I am certain that clothes are a reflection of character.

Show me a man's top-hat and I'll give a good guess at his ideas ; show me a woman's hat and I am utterly dumbfounded.

I suppose in ten years' time we shall have swept away many of these traces I have just explained ; that we shall have succumbed even more to the deadening effect of this mechanical age which seems to have utterly exhausted our power of invention for anything but electricity and instruments of destruction ; and that photographs of ourselves will look laughable and wonderfully old-fashioned and our clothes queer and ill-suited to men even as do those we look back on now, though it seems to me that there was some glory in the big stocks and rolled collars, in the strapped trousers and fine fobs that we miss in our neutral, rather sloppy times. However, it is interesting to think that even the end of the world will hear the steady snip of the cutter's scissors.

From "Etcetera"

THE ENGLISH ESSAYIST

JOHN FREEMAN

I

MR SAINTSBURY'S phrase, " Works of prose art," lingers on the mind as the definition of Bacon's best work and a generalization of the essay itself. Split and refine it as we may, it has still an essential truth ; the essay is a piece of prose art, and when we have marked its chief distinctions and pursued its main diversions we shall find that its development has been towards a finer order, a more conscious art, a heightening and ultimately a completer fusion of those twin faculties of the mind, imagination and reason.

The essay comes somewhat slowly into the story of English letters. Romantic narrative, miracle play, drama—these confusedly preceded, and the essay followed with an uncertain apprehension of the aims and powers of those other forms ; and clearly the essay could have no place until the first exuberance of invention and imagination had passed, and men began to rub their eyes and look a little narrowly at what had been achieved and at what was left to do. Yet the essay has seldom been solely critical in any age, and in noting this we approach the first fork in our road ; on one side the merely critical, the slightly curious or slightly arid abstraction—moral or æsthetic —and on the other the more serenely imaginative and mobile form which later ages were to bring to full development. Bacon's *Essays* belong to the moral and intellectual division, though not exclusively to that ; the pregnancy of his phrase, his voluptuous verbal beauty and purely sensuous indulgences, noticeable in so many passages of music and solid colour, are a token that his was indeed a complex spirit. Nevertheless, the real preoccupation of his essays is not sensuous or æsthetic, but moral and rational. Ask what is the most characteristic expression in Elizabethan letters of the mind of a liberal scholar, and the answer will probably be Bacon's *Essays*. Sedate and grave in his thoughts, splendid in his mode, he loves to invest his inspired and commonplace utterances alike in a gorgeous cloak. *Decadent!* a paradoxical writer might murmur as he notes the frequent overweighting of the idea by the expression, and reminds us thereby that decadence in literature is somewhat older than the already antique nineties at which we glance with amusement, anon with contempt. Bacon's commonplaces, looked at closely, are among the worst, being moral commonplaces—midgetary moralities augustly presented and speaking big. But it was not simply his delight in splendour which urged his noblest phrasing, it was equally his desire to use the magnificence of his time in the service of reason and order.

We are helped in thus seeing Francis Bacon, Lord Verulam, by the familiar portrait which so comprehensively tells us the truth, the whole truth, and nothing but the truth about our author. The gravity is there, the weighty preoccupation, the slyness of after-thoughts unexpressed, the richness of tone and hue—all these are seen more and more plainly as you stare back at his stare ; and they are qualities that make him an essayist of real interest to the lightest as well as the profoundest reader. But they also make him a particular kind of essayist—not an intimate but a reserved figure, not a talker but a writer, not a babbler but a rhetorician, not a companion but a teacher, not a friend but a great chancellor, not a familiar forgetting his dignity but a supple statesman asserting it ; preferring to suppress, equivocate, and dissemble, and to justify every obliquity—anything rather than candidly pour himself out and leave the justification to the reader. The experience of a lifetime is the well from which his *aurea dicta* are solemnly drawn ; and who does not know the varied kinds of Bacon's experience ? *Corruptions' Nuncio* we might call him, thinking of his sins and splendours, his meanness and magniloquence. He writes a whole essay " Of Cunning," beginning by a distinction between cunning and wisdom and forgetting the distinction long before he ends, the essay becoming a half-candid apology for cunning ; he writes a sombre and noble eulogy of death, spending all he has in adorning those commonplaces that are never staled ; but one thing he never attempts to do, rather does he avoid it—he never speaks out from the tiny callous kernel of his heart. It is not the true spendthrift of himself who writes : " Nakedness is uncomely as well in mind as in body ; and it addeth no small reverence to men's names, manners, and actions, if they be not altogether open " ; and in the same essay proceeds to vindicate simulation and dissimulation. The intellectual spendthrift is the true essayist, if only he have enough of himself to spend ; but Bacon was a miser of himself, sitting furred and gilded and cold, like some gorgeous Renaissance figure of a dusky painting, counting over his gains with pursed lips and sidelong eye, his fingers trembling, jewels flash-

ing, and lips shaping a careful phrase for the enrich-
ment of hungry Time.

He may have taught Ben Jonson, a slightly younger
man, the secret of sententiousness, or at least its value,
as well as the use of the flower-like decoration of
simple prose ; for Bacon himself might be heard in
the closing note of this from the *Discoveries* : " What
a deal of cold business doth a man misspend the better
part of life in ! in scattering compliments, tendering
visits, gathering and venting news, following feasts
and plays, making a little winter love in a dark
corner." Conciseness is his aim, in a degree that
even Bacon never cared for, and all the weightiness of
the penurious chancellor is found in these little essays
of his thriftless contemporary. If, however, Jonson's
style offers reminders of the greater essayist, it presents differences far more positive. He empties himself prodigally before you and does not scruple to tell
precisely those things which Bacon hid. The conversations at Hawthornden, as related by Drummond,
reveal sharply enough his huge sense of his own worth
and others' worthlessness, for nothing that is not Ben
Jonson's pleases him freely, and there is mere cur-
rishness in his constant diminution of every figure
within his recollection ; but in the *Discoveries* his
freedoms are pleasanter. He still sneers, and sneers
even at Montaigne for an essayist ; but happily he
is more truly at ease when he speaks of his own life.
Not for Jonson any vaunting or practice of dissimulation. " At last they upbraided my poverty. I
confess she is my Domestic, sober of diet, simple of
habit, frugal, painful ; a good Counsellor to me, that
keeps me from Cruelty, Pride, or other more delicate impertinences which are the Nurse-children of
Riches." He writes an essay on " Style," and still it

is of Ben Jonson he writes, saying how he loves a pure and neat language, how often a barbarous phrase has made him out of love with good sense ; their writings need sunshine, he cries, as he thinks of delinquent authors. Himself dominates his writings, and consequently you are aware of that vivacious figure, that Stentor voice of authority, that rude yet delicate power of picture, that fond assertion of his own tastes, which we faintly conjure up when we look on any portrait of Jonson. He gibes at Montaigne, but follows him.

II

Many of the authors of what is conveniently called miscellaneous prose, in the years succeeding Jonson's death, are strictly essayists, and of all the truest essayist and finest master of our medium was Sir Thomas Browne. It is unnecessary to point out that he too takes a place in our second and more native class of essayist—those who follow the imaginative and mobile personal form. Browne plays upon his own being like a splendid musician who is able to evoke the solemn and the playful, the wise and the tender, from the depths and shallows of his inward life ; and then, turning to a vaster instrument, with equal serenity he summons the august, dreadful yet unoppressive echo-voices of death and time. Now 'tis like all instruments, now like a lonely flute. In the midst of the largest of his generalizations you never lose sight of himself ; in his most fantastic speculations a clear-smiling grave spirit is distinct and individual. Shut your eyes as a phrase from *Urn Burial* or *Religio Medici* unfolds upon the air, and you see at once the courtly, masculine face, the eyes of smouldering fancies and passionate, tranquil curiosity that make Sir Thomas Browne living and dear more than dead and remembered. Does he write for any but himself? true essayist, it is thus that he writes for us. After three centuries we should be little engrossed in any writer who is not engrossed in himself. Ideas may attract, history and science may touch a faded figure with spectral incandescence, but only that which is human lives on in human affections. It is a pitiful truism to say that Browne's primary quality is Browne. Seventeenth-century morals (whether Christian or non-Christian), cinerary rites—these would not of themselves distract the twentieth century from thinking of its own morals and incineration ; but Browne has done something with the essay which no other writer has done so potently—he has deepened the form as an English tradition and exalted it as an English art. " Vain ashes," he writes—" Vain ashes, which in the oblivion of names, persons, times and sexes, have found unto themselves a fruitless continuation, and only arise unto late posterity as Emblems of mortal vanities, Antidotes against pride, vainglory, and madding vices." It is singular enough that his own skull should have been gnawed out of the grave—a fate that he shrank from as a " tragical abomination " ; but is it an antidote against pride ? Would he have been humbled to know it, or provoked to a new and yet more gorgeous dehortation upon chance, and the insecurity of death ? And for ourselves, we peer at his pages for a sight of him, and we find his skull at our feet. Gentlest of mockeries !

III

In pursuing our theme along these not too densely
hedged paths, we must not be beguiled into mere
vague extension, else we should be sweeping all the
pamphleteers that succeeded Browne into our narrow
scope. The pamphlet is not an essay except by a
fortunate accident, and the air of dispute and violent
wrangling amid which the pamphleteer's voice is
heard is not the air in which literature survives when
the subject of contention is itself burnt out.   Dryden
is one who outrides the dispute he engaged in, but in
citing Dryden here I am naming simply the chief
and not the sole late seventeenth-century essayist,
and first if not the chief of those who practised purely
critical writing. The famous *Essay of Dramatic Poesie*,
born of a dispute with Sir Robert Howard and giving
birth in turn to other provocative treatises, is the
admired example of the best work of the critical kind,
and it followed hard upon an essay which, for other
qualities, deserves nearly as much praise—Cowley's
Discourse Concerning Oliver Cromwell. In each case
there is reason harnessed to imagination, a criticism
of affairs or a criticism of ideas ; each is a work of
prose art, each shows a beautiful art of prose.   The
chief difference between Jonson and Browne on one
side, and Cowley and Dryden on the other, is that
the latter do not speak so freely of themselves ; they
are not involuntary revealers of their own business
and bosoms, they are not portrait artists, they are not
their own texts.   If therefore they lose or refrain from
the last charm, it must be owned that they do not
pretend to it.   You cannot read Dryden's very features
into his *Dramatic Poesy*, and, Dryden being Dryden,
it is to be doubted whether that essay would be better

if you could. He has much, but not *that* charm, not *that* power over us ; while Cowley has powers of humour, satire, and an admiring scorn, but not the gift of showing in a few brief pages the shape and shadow of his inward being ; he does not step out of or even into his own pages and set them shaking in our hand. Dryden's intellectual force could not but make itself everywhere apparent in his *Dramatic Poesy*, but this is a mere general quality, not a personal and identifiable characteristic ; and general qualities may exist in abundance, yet the personal features, the human lineaments, faculties, and humours remain vague and uncomposed. But, as we have said, Dryden was doing one kind and not another kind of thing —the intellectual, the critical essay, the essay of ideas, the essay which ought to be understandable almost as well in French as in English. And this indeed points to a quick test, for the essay of the singularly personal kind, the essay of self-portraiture (whether quite involuntary or quite deliberate), as Browne and Lamb used it, is perhaps inevitably untranslatable. Our homage, nevertheless, can be offered to Dryden as the father of that " criticism of ideas " which critics of our day deplore the want of and which, indeed, our literary tradition seems natively incapable of begetting. What Dryden himself can give us is this intellectual criticism in a prose which delights us in its own way scarcely less than Jonson's in another. It is a prose that fits its subject like a glove, like the skin to the flesh of the hand ; but at times its rational strictness is broken and the phrases leap :

MY LORD,
This worthless present was designed you, long before it was a Play ; when it was only a confused mass of thoughts tumbling over one another in the dark : when the Fancy

was yet in its first work, moving the sleeping Images of Things towards the light, there to be distinguished ; and then, either chosen or rejected by the Judgement. It was yours, My Lord ! before I could call it mine.

If Dryden told cousin Swift that he would never be a poet, as he is supposed to have said, he could not have told him he would never be a prose writer. Swift's prose was miscellaneous enough, but he does not permit us to confine him within our notion of essays, and if he can fairly be called an essayist it is mainly because he was one of the begetters of another kind of essay—the periodical essay—the light-armed, light-headed infantry of prose literature ; and might we but add light-hearted, that would indeed be final praise, but except in the Roger de Coverley series it had no heart at all. Truth reminds us, however, that Swift was begetting something far unlike himself, far different from his own sombre and burdened imaginations. Here, in the prattling shallows of Addison's wit, in the gay impulses of Steele's good-nature, in the light, neat, sociable prose of both, the new kind of essay was created in sudden perfection. Literature as a handmaid, waiting-wench to fashion, conventions, morals, mere dresser to a patched and painted actress, or moving among the teacups and gossips of a society in which it seemeth always afternoon—these are the new offices to which imagination and ' wit ' are subdued. Genius has come to town and put off its native rudeness and power, and put on urban airs and graces, the airs of a flirt in a metropolis that has just discovered the meaning of ' polite ' and ' charming,' the graces of an impertinent dependent. There is masterly portraiture in the *Spectator* and *Tatler*, delicate engraving, faint felicities of pencil and needle, but it is rather a portraiture of society than of the artists themselves ; they are sunken in the crowd for which they speak, they are not the perfect egotists who are to be identified with the perfect essayists. It is perhaps not very strange that the age in which everybody wrote essays and the form was sharpened for the use of the society just finding its feet or its head, was an age in which a level was reached and the peaks sank to the level. When all wrote well none wrote supremely.

IV

It is to Johnson that we must look for supremacy in another kind, and to Goldsmith for a gift as unique as Johnson's if less powerful. Johnson made a new thing when he followed the periodical essay of the *Rambler* with the mature improvisations—it is their charm that they are scarcely more—of *The Lives of the Poets*. They form the model of the biographical essay, in which the features of the subject are drawn sometimes minutely and sometimes freely, and behind these the features of the writer himself, the avowed portrait dimming away into the careless and unconscious portrait of the artist ; or if the self-portraiture is less unstudied, as in that beautiful tribute to Gilbert Walmsley occurring in the life of Smith, it is no whit less delightful. Johnson's large and eloquent personality continually overflowed, and on the waves the light and fragile memories of the immemorable, the Smiths and Dukes and Sprats of his fortuitous collection, floated securely. It is only because so many have tried their nervous hands at the biographical essay, in artless imitation, that Johnson's work is not unique ; but it is still unapproached.

And so we might turn to Goldsmith, deliciously satirical, the most innocent of men, writing his *Citizen of the World* as though he were standing outside the world and looking on amused ; ostensibly following the critical type of our classification, but with imagination continually breaking through. The shadow of the pathetic which has always been cast on Goldsmith's figure, heaven knows why, by writers on his time, has obscured some of his independent merits, and the *Citizen* has been stupidly overlooked because its author has been sentimentalized. From Goldsmith, again, it is a single flying leap to Lamb and Hazlitt, and a new development of the essay. Imagination continually breaking through might be said of Lamb also, but I do not pretend to define Lamb's mode. Lamb is no Lamb but a thing of nimbler nature—sometimes a mocking cuckoo, sometimes a wise white owl, blinking his enormous golden orbs against an intrusive light and whirring into the soft dusky privacy of the mind ; sometimes a robin, friendliest of domestic voices, kindest of winter's colours ; and sometimes a rich-throated blackbird flitting with his prose elegies about the graves of the poets he loved—Sidney and Cotton and Coleridge and the rest ; the purest of egotists, the most candid of self-revealers, the best loved of all lovers. It is easier, though hardly more useful, to find a metaphor for Hazlitt—that vigorous, restless, watchful, and growling hound, who barks out his short, crisp sentences, snaps here, fondles there, never sleeps, has a merry eye for a few and a flashing eye for most, flings himself with wild fangs upon a Gifford and heaves at last with angry gratification. He, too, is his own eternal subject ; his essays are the irritable plate on which his features have been recorded, both

consciously and unconsciously, during long years of
self-communion. Extravagancies of metaphor, however, are to be avoided, and we may leave Hazlitt
(never quite adequately admired), and stay scarce a
moment to mark De Quincey's intricate confusion of
sound with colour, the rich hues wreathed in cloud,
in those disorderly conceptions which at once fascinate
and fatigue us, and prove that in him one of the
greatest essayists was strangled, alas, and not fulfilled
—an impish and unstable figure playing upon his
own fantastic personality as though it were another's.
We may leave, too, the *Quarterly* and *Edinburgh*
reviewers of his day, by whom the essay was more
and more steadily reduced to journalism, sometimes
critical, sometimes dishonest, sometimes merely un-
critical ; but we cannot so easily leave his impressive
contemporary Landor, who achieved a new form for
the essay when he wrote and rewrote his all but
endless *Imaginary Conversations*, mingling by mere hap
the imaginative and the rational in capricious proportion and using a prose that no one since has
bettered. Yet it would be foolish to attempt the
definition of Landor's mode or the praise of his style,
that can be dull when the subject is tedious, and
serene and noble when the theme is right. With
Landor it is not enough that he should write of himself, for even then he is sometimes merely solemn and
garrulous, and perhaps he needs the warmth of a
mental opposition ; but his best passages may occur
almost anywhere, and include such phrasing as this
that echoes along the vaulting of the senses :

" He who hath lived in this country, can enjoy no
distant one. He breathes here another air ; he lives
more life ; a brighter sun invigorates his studies, and
serener stars influence his repose. Barbary hath also

the blessing of climate ; and although I do not desire
to be there again, I sometimes feel a kind of regret
at leaving it. A bell warbles the more mellifluously
in the air when the sound of the stroke is over, and
when another swims out from underneath it, and
pants upon the element that gave it birth. In like
manner the recollection of a thing is frequently more
pleasing than the actuality ; what is harsh is dropped
in the space between."

Landor might have told more of himself if he had
been less sharply aware of himself and had cared less
to support an ideal disdain which we cannot wholly
admire ; but he is still an essayist of the true personal
order, still the self-portrayer, with a restless world
sinking into sullen cloud behind his briefly tran-
quillized figure.

But injustice will yet be done if we pursue this
light-heeled journey with no more than an unre-
flecting glance at Matthew Arnold, and forget the
sallies that shook, or at least vexed, the intellectual
world of fifty years ago. Arnold enjoyed the air of
dispute and was never so happy as in asserting that
others were wrong and foolish and perturbed about
nothing, and thus he hangs half-way between the
critical and the personal, friendlier than he cares to
show, yet guarding his inward flame somewhat too
jealously from the casual breath of others. And in
speaking of Arnold, as of Walter Pater, the reference
is likely to sound purely and completely one of personal fondness, the regard for Pater especially being
grounded partly upon a sympathy with his general
æsthetic attitude, and partly upon an admiration of
his silent, smouldering passion of English prose. The
sympathy and the admiration alike are nourished by
" Sebastian Van Storck " and the rest of his *Imaginary*

Portraits, as well as those many essays, long or short, from *Marius* to the child in the house, wherein Pater is disclosing, in subdued and burning hue, the movement of his sense-exalted, sense-confounded spirit.

These I cannot linger over ; they are chiefly essayists of the imaginative division, and when they touch criticism it is of the order that a few stern readers abhor and most admire, being a result of the confronting of their own and their subjects' personalities, the opposition of their stars or the conjunction of their loves. Precisely the same thing is to be seen in others of their time and later, in Coventry Patmore and Alice Meynell, and in certain living writers who practise an honoured art and remember that it is an art, a service, and a dignity—I refer to Mr George Moore and Mr Max Beerbohm ; and in speaking of these latter writers, I remember first of all that they have achieved felicity irrespective of a lucky choice of subject. Like a dim-silked, dark-hued Mandarin, moving amid the strange confusion of an Occidental procession, " Max " keeps a fine reserve that is itself more expressive than others' loquacity, and achieves the last distinction by forbearance, elision, and a civil avoidance of paunchy superfluity. But Mr Moore—I find no single similitude for him. The chameleon is not more changeable, the snake with his annual sloughing of faded vesture is not more subtly renewed, the cock that crows against the sun lifts no prouder head, the stoat has not slyer motion, the kestrel no more watchful eye nor idler-seeming pose, the wandering mew no lonelier note nor her shadow a briefer visitation, than Mr George Moore in the abundant prose that began, for our purpose, in *Essays and Opinions* and grew perfect a generation

R

later in *Avowals*. To gloat over these, co-rivals and twin incomparables, would be to forgo the pleasure of pondering even a brief word upon others of our day who, like them, have given of their best to this winning and wanton form : wanton, it may be called, because it is the peculiar form in which the mind independently roams, sinks and soars, and pursues its delightful porpoise-way through territorial waters. The essayist that lately died with W. H. Hudson is an example of one kind, the essayist that continually renews a sprightly youth in Mr Saintsbury is another kind, and between the two there are how many contemporaries, critical or imaginative, strict or desultory, for whose lightest page we are all grateful. Hudson identified himself with his subject and thereby the more completely and purely expressed himself ; Mr Saintsbury, in his *Scrap Books* (for example) of the last few years, has given us something almost unique in its careless fulness, its readiness of resource, its Johnsonian echo of humorous and sane dogmatism.

v

But here the boldest of writers must pause, when he finds himself among contemporaries who are plainly of the elect company of their predecessors, and especially if he has looked even a little critically at some and indulgently at others, avowing thereby his own likings more than any abstract standard of judgment. The phrase used by a modern poet, Mr W. H. Davies, " short men that sit tall," may be adopted to describe the aspiring humbleness that befits such a writer, as he looks out upon his world. Thorns outline the fields, and there is indeed as much of rebuke as of stimulation in the view, sting and sweetness equally palpable. But no man can be forbidden the indulgence of his own thoughts, and criticism is subdued in pleasure when the English essay is followed from the time of Queen Elizabeth down to our own vivid and voracious day. If pleasure is then my only excuse, it may be stated boldly that no other is needed and a cat may still look at a king if only he refrain from snarling at kingship and kingdoms ; a task or pastime for which I have not the least inclination.

My simple theme, then, reiterated to tediousness but now concluded, is that the mere egotism of the author, freely confessed or subtly dissembled, forms the chief delight of the English essay. Musing upon his own thoughts and instincts, upon whatever in himself is powerful though inarticulate, upon his own passions and humours, the true essayist awakes in his readers the admiration of a soldier for his captain, the fondness of a lover for his last beloved. Intimacies stir and run out beneath the common soil, experience rains down and quickens the roots, and the thoughts of the author at length become the thoughts of the reader, his passions become our passions, his humours ours, his virtues and follies ours ; for the main concern of any reader is with the author himself, and there is no bond so secure, no link so unrusting, as this that gleams between them. The literature of the last hundred years has seen the triumph of the novel, vast satrapies overrun and a border-war with science beginning, like that deadly Flanders war of trench and gas ; and the essay has been left unattempted by alert spirits that might have won. Nevertheless, the essay lives and thrives. Resuming metaphor for the last time it may be said that, like a huge oak, whose guttered trunk and fungus'd shoulder darkens the hill, the English novel stands boldly yet, his thin hair shaking in the cold winds ; but the essay is like a thicket, changing and never dying, with dusks and deeps within, refuge of birds and shy wild beasts, home of strange and familiar voices.

From "English Portraits and Essays"

INDEX OF AUTHORS